ADDISON-WESLEY COMPUTER-BASED

WordPerfect®
VERSION 6 FOR WINDOWS™

Matthew Nowicki
844-7133

ADDISON-WESLEY COMPUTER-BASED LEARNING SERIES

WordPerfect®
VERSION 6 FOR WINDOWS™

Bob Lewis, *Sheridan College*

Eugene J. Rathswohl
James T. Perry
Ahmer S. Karim
University of San Diego

Integrating computer-based instruction software developed by:
American Training International

 Addison-Wesley Publishers Limited

Don Mills, Ontario • Reading, Massachusetts
Menlo Park, California • New York • Wokingham, England
Amsterdam • Bonn • Sydney • Tokyo • Madrid • San Juan

Canadian Cataloguing in Publication Data

Main entry under title:

WordPerfect 6.0 for Windows

(Addison-Wesley computer based learning series)
Includes index.
ISBN 0-201-83709-9

1. WordPerfect for Windows (Computer file).   2. Word processing – Computer programs.   I. Lewis, Bob, 1946–   .   II. Series

Z52.5.W655W67   1995   652.5'5369   C95-931109–2

Copyright © 1995 Addison-Wesley Publishers Limited

Much of the material in this publication was first published in *WordPerfect® 6 Projects for Windows™* by Eugene J. Rathswohl, James T. Perry, and Ahmer S. Karim (The Benjamin/Cummings Publishing Company, Inc., © 1995).

The author and publisher have taken care in the preparation of this book, but make no expressed or implied warranty of any kind and assume no responsibility for errors or omissions. No liability is assumed for accidental or consequential damages in connection with or arising out of the use of the information contained herein.

All rights reserved. No part of this publication may be reproduced, or stored in a database or retrieval system, distributed, or transmitted in any form or by any means, electronic, mechanical, photocopying, recording or otherwise without the prior written permission of the publisher.

ISBN 0-201-83709-9

Printed in Canada.

B C D E MP 99 98 97

TRADEMARKS

WordPerfect is the registered trademark of WordPerfect Corporation.
Windows is the registered trademark of Microsoft Corporation.

BASIS is the trademark of Robert A. Lewis. Licensed for use with this publication by Addison-Wesley Publishers Limited.

Contents

INTRODUCTION TO THE *BASIS* MODULES *vii*

INTRODUCTION TO WINDOWS *xi*

INTRODUCTION TO WORDPERFECT 6 FOR WINDOWS *1*
  Getting Started *2*
  Topic Objectives *2*
  Computer Tutorial *3*
  Practice Exercises *4*
    Using a Word Processor *5*
    Using WordPerfect 6 for Windows *6*
    Starting WordPerfect 6 for Windows *7*
    Using the Document Window *8*
    Using WordPerfect Commands *10*
      Choosing Menu Options Using the Mouse *10*
      Using the Keyboard and Keystroke Combinations *11*
      Cancelling and Undoing Commands *11*
      Using the Power Bar and the Button Bar *12*
      Using Dialog Boxes *12*
    Getting Online Help *15*
      Context-Sensitive Help *17*
      WordPerfect Help Features *17*
    Exiting WordPerfect 6 for Windows *19*
    Summary *19*
    Key Terms and Operations *20*
    Study Questions *20*
  Competency Testing *21*

CREATING A DOCUMENT *22*
  Topic Objectives *22*
  Computer Tutorial *22*
  Practice Exercises *22*
    Project 1: Creating a Document 23
      Case Study: Writing a Job Application Letter *23*
      Designing the Solution *23*
      Entering Text *25*
      Moving Around in the Document *26*
      Making Simple Corrections *28*
      Saving the Document *30*
      Previewing the Document *32*
      Printing the Document *34*
      Exiting the Current Document *35*
      The Next Step *35*
      Summary *36*
      Key Terms and Operations *36*
      Study Questions *37*
      Review Exercises *38*
  Competency Testing *40*

EDITING THE DOCUMENT *41*
  Topic Objectives *41*
  Computer Tutorial *41*
  Practice Exercises *42*
    Project 2: Editing the Document 42
      Case Study: Writing a Newspaper Article *42*
      Designing the Solution *42*
      Opening a Document *43*
      Saving the Document Under a Different Name *45*
      Finding and Replacing Text *47*
      Using the WordPerfect Speller *50*
      Using the Thesaurus *52*
      Selecting Text *54*
      Deleting Blocks of Text *55*
      Moving and Copying Blocks of Text *56*
      The Next Step *58*
      Summary *58*
      Key Terms and Operations *59*
      Study Questions *59*
      Review Exercises *61*
  Competency Testing *62*

FORMATTING THE DOCUMENT *63*
  Topic Objectives *63*
  Computer Tutorial *63*
  Practice Exercises *63*
    Project 3: Formatting the Document 64
      Case Study: Formatting an Announcement *64*
      Designing the Solution *64*
      Revealing Formatting Codes *66*
      Using the Ruler Bar *68*
      Setting Margins *69*
      Justifying Text *71*
      Setting Tabs *75*
        Clearing Existing Tabs *77*
        Setting New Tabs *78*
      Indenting Text *81*
      Setting Line Spacing *83*
      Forcing a New Page *84*
      The Next Step *86*
      Summary *86*
      Key Terms and Operations *87*
      Study Questions *87*
      Review Exercises *89*
  Competency Testing *91*

ENHANCING THE DOCUMENT 92
    Topic Objectives 92
    Computer Tutorial 92
    Practice Exercises 92
        Project 4: Enhancing the Document 93
            Case Study: Enhancing a Class Handout 93
                Designing the Solution 93
            Changing Typeface and Type Size 96
            Boldfacing, Underlining,
             and Italicizing Text 97
            Using Special Character Sets 98
            Numbering Pages 100
            Adding Headers and Footers 102
            Adding Footnotes and Endnotes 104
            The Next Step 106
            Summary 107
            Key Terms and Operations 107
            Study Questions 107
            Review Exercises 109
    Competency Testing 110

COMPETENCY TEST PREPARATION AND SUMMARY 111
    Competency Test Preparation 111
    Module Objectives 111
    Computer Tutorial 112
    Competency Testing 113
    Summary 114

    Operations Reference 116
    Glossary 127
    Index 133

Introduction to the *BASIS*™ Modules

The Basic Academic Skills - Independent Study (*BASIS*) system is designed to help you develop some of the foundation skills you will need in your post-secondary training and in your future career.

Computers are playing an ever-increasing role in the workplace, and the *BASIS* Computer Applications series of modules emphasizes the skills most in demand.

All *BASIS* modules have the same format:

   STEP 1   Computer-based tutorials

   STEP 2   Structured practice exercises

   STEP 3   Competency testing

BASIS modules are easy to use. You start with the first computer-based tutorial, after which you work your way through related practice exercises. You then return to the next tutorial and its related practice exercises, and so on until you have finished all the training. To complete the module you attempt a competency test, which measures the skills you have acquired.

Before you start this *BASIS* module, it is very important that you read through:

- the introductory material (pp. viii to x)
- your *BASIS* **User's Guide**[1]

If you are new to Windows, it is also important that you read through the following material before beginning the module:

- **Introduction to Windows** (pp. xi to xxix)

Welcome to the *BASIS* system, and good luck!

---

[1] **A *BASIS* User's Guide** may not be used at all institutions and/or another term may be used to refer to it at your institution (e.g., "*BASIS* Student Manual").

Format of Modules

All *BASIS* modules follow the same format:

- Every module is divided into major topics.

    Each major topic starts with a box exactly like the one on page 1.

- Each topic contains four sections:

    - Topic Objectives
    - Computer Tutorial
    - Practice Exercises
    - Competency Testing

These sections are identified by the following icons:

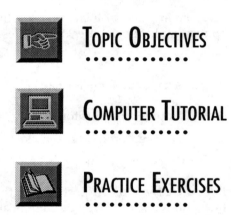

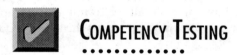

The sections are laid out in a logical and carefully designed sequence. *We strongly recommend that you do work in the order in which it is presented in modules.* Skipping around may lead to confusion and/or unnecessary mistakes, both of which are needlessly time-consuming. You will detect some repetition of specific tasks between sections. This is intentional: skills are only learned and developed by practice.

Pages ix and x outline the four sections in greater detail.

Sections Within Each Topic

Topic Objectives

Every major topic in a *BASIS* module begins with a list of topic objectives. *You should always read the topic objectives before beginning a major topic.*

Topic objectives outline for you:

- What you should learn from working through the topic.
- What you should expect to be able to demonstrate on the competency test.

The **Topic Objectives** section within each major topic outlines for you exactly what the objectives are for that major topic.

Computer Tutorial

BASIS computer tutorials take you through material that shows you how to meet each of the objectives outlined in the Topic Objectives.

The computer tutorials are interactive: you just follow on-screen explanations and instructions, then enter information or press various keys when you're asked to do so. The tutorial program won't let you press the wrong buttons, so don't worry about making mistakes. The computer tutorials often include practice exercises, and always review all material covered.

The computer tutorials provide the major instruction for all *BASIS* modules. Therefore, in order to be fully prepared for the competency test for that module, it is your responsibility to:

- Do all assigned computer tutorial material.
- Do all recommended practice material within the computer tutorial.
- Make notes for yourself where you feel it is necessary for you to do so to fully understand the material covered.
- Repeat material you do not understand the first time.

The **Computer Tutorial** section within each major topic outlines for you exactly which parts of the computer tutorial you are supposed to do for that major topic.

Practice Exercises

Practice exercises help you strengthen your understanding of concepts covered in the related computer tutorial. In a few instances, explanatory material will be introduced in the Practice Exercises section only and not in the computer tutorial. On those occasions when objectives are met through material in only one place (the computer tutorial or the practice exercises), that fact will be highlighted in the Topic Objectives.

There are three parts to the practice exercises for each major topic:

- **Projects** — A series of small, specific projects written as command-based instruction. These projects, together, lead to completion of a larger project.
- **Study Questions** — Short exercises to be used as self-tests to help you measure your progress.
- **Review Exercises** — Hands-on tasks with numbered steps. These "abbreviated" instructions (without specific commands shown) help you build on skills learned in the topic without "leading" you step by step.

The **Practice Exercises** section within each major topic outlines for you exactly which projects, study questions, and review exercises you are supposed to do for that major topic.

Competency Testing

The competency test for each *BASIS* module is a comprehensive, hands-on test of approximately 45 to 60 minutes duration. (There is a short written portion on Windows in the test for the DOS/Windows modules.) It is designed to measure your competency with respect to *all topic objectives combined*.

In order to qualify to write the competency test for any given *BASIS* module, you must have completed *all* practice exercises associated with *all* topics for that module.

The **Competency Testing** section within each major topic outlines for you exactly which projects, study questions, and review exercises you must have completed for that major topic in order to qualify to write the competency test for the module.

Introduction to Windows

Objectives

In this introduction, you will learn how to:

- Use a mouse.
- Start and exit Windows.
- Get help in Windows.
- Access the Program Manager menu and the Control menu.
- Use a dialog box.
- Manipulate windows and icons.
- Start and exit a program.

Since the introduction of computers in the 1940s, an evolution has occurred. Operations such as saving, loading, and running a program on early computers required an extraordinary degree of knowledge and the skills of a specialist. After the 1950s, these same tasks were performed by operating systems, groups of programs that control and supervise the computer system operations. Since the introduction of graphical user interfaces in the 1980s, computers work on the user's terms. Even computer novices can quickly learn to use the visual display of these "user friendly" environments.

Using Windows 3.1

An *operating system* is a complex set of instructions that manages a computer's resources. Windows 3.1 is a full-featured graphical operating environment that greatly extends the capabilities of DOS, IBM's disk operating system. Windows is not an operating system, but an operating environment that runs "on top of" DOS. First you load DOS, and then you load Windows. Application programs, such as Microsoft Excel and Microsoft Word, are then loaded under Windows.

The DOS command line is replaced with a *graphical user interface (GUI)* that is much easier to learn than DOS's text-based interface. The Windows *desktop* (the screen background) serves as a graphical-based work area (see Figure 1). Application programs and documents are found inside different *windows* (rectangular areas on the desktop). In a graphical user interface, operations are executed by selecting *icons,* graphical representations of Windows elements, and by choosing options from lists of commands called *menus*. For example, to copy a disk, you choose the Copy Disk command from the Disk menu.

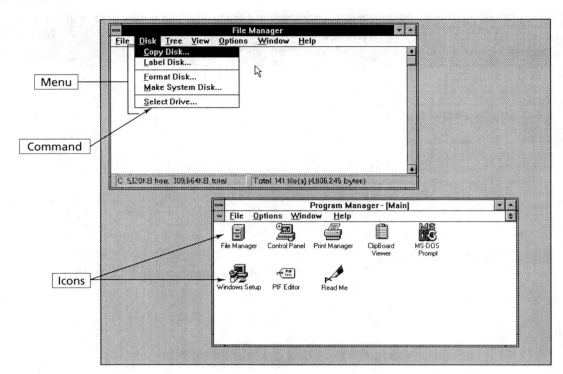

Figure 1

To take full advantage of all of the features in Windows 3.1, you must buy special versions of software programs, known as *Windows applications.* When you buy an application software package, the product's box will indicate whether it has been written specifically for Windows. This does not mean that only Windows applications can run under Windows. Almost all programs run under Windows, but *non-Windows applications,* programs not designed specifically for Windows, cannot take advantage of many of Windows' features.

A NOTE TO THE STUDENT

The instructions in the projects describe how to execute commands with a mouse. Comparable keyboard keystrokes are included for computer systems without a mouse. For example, a typical instruction will look like:

1. Mouse: Click File on the menu bar.
   or Keys: Press ALT + **F**

Refer to the *Getting Started* section for a detailed explanation of how keystrokes are presented in the module.

Using a Mouse

Windows 3.1 is designed to be used with a pointing device such as a mouse or trackball. A *mouse* is a hand-held input device that is rolled on a small flat surface, usually a table or mouse pad. The movement of the mouse causes a corresponding movement of a pointer on the screen. A *trackball* performs the same function as a mouse but works somewhat differently. You use your fingers to roll a ball that is exposed on the top of the device, which causes the pointer to move on the screen.

There are several common terms that you need to know when using a mouse. The *pointer* is a symbol (usually an arrow) that moves around the screen as you move your mouse. To *click* means to position the pointer on an object and then quickly press and release the left mouse button. A *double-click* involves the same motion as a click, but the mouse button is pressed and released twice in rapid succession. Usually this causes a small hourglass icon to appear on the screen for a few seconds. The hourglass indicates that you need to wait while Windows loads something. When you *drag* an object, you will hold down the left mouse button while moving the mouse. Dragging is used for moving or sizing an object or choosing commands.

The *menu bar* lists available menus. An application usually has File, Edit, and Help menus, in addition to the application's unique menus. To use a mouse to choose a command, you will click the name of the menu on the menu bar. A *drop-down menu,* a menu that drops down onto the screen, will appear, as shown in Figure 2. While holding down the left mouse button, you will highlight the desired command and then release the button to execute the command. Alternatively, you can execute a command by clicking the command in the drop-down menu.

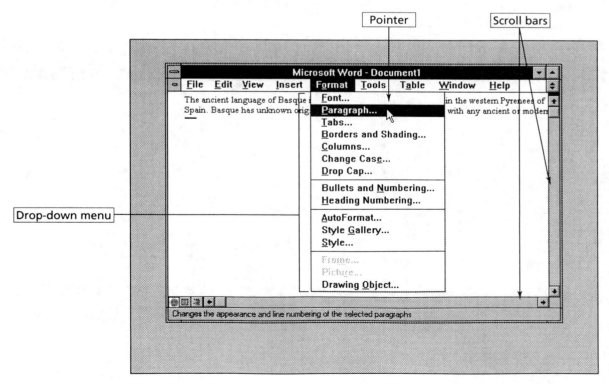

Figure 2

Some windows have bars, called *scroll bars,* along the right and/or bottom border. Figure 2 displays scroll bars for scrolling through a document. You can move through the document or the list of choices one line at a time by clicking either arrow at the end of the scroll bar. You can move to a specific location by dragging the *scroll box,* the box within the scroll bar. You can also scroll with the keyboard one line at a time by pressing ↓ and ↑ or one screen at a time by pressing PGUP and PGDN .

STARTING AND EXITING WINDOWS

The following steps describe the standard method for starting Windows. Before you can begin, DOS must be installed in the computer. But since DOS is typically installed with hard disk and networked systems, you only need to turn on the computer's power.

How you start Windows itself depends on how your computer is set up. For example, your computer may be running a menu system or the DOS Shell that facilitates the starting of Windows. A typical setup is for a computer screen to display the DOS prompt, which is a letter followed by a > sign. A> and B> are used for floppy disk systems, C> for hard disk systems, and F> for network systems.

➤ To start Windows:

1. Type **win** at the DOS prompt and press ENTER

   The first screen to appear is the Windows 3.1 logo, which is soon followed by a window called the Program Manager. Your screen may look a little different from the one in Figure 3.

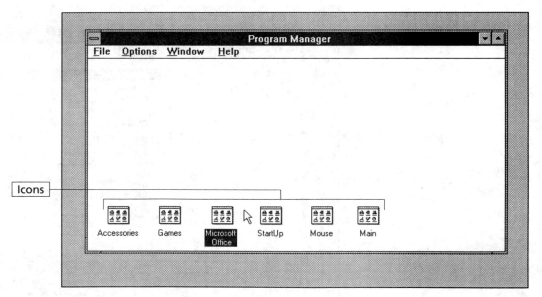

Figure 3

INTRODUCTION TO WINDOWS

➤ **To exit Windows:**

1. Mouse: Click File on the menu bar.
   or Keys: Press [ALT] + **F**

   Your screen should look like the one in Figure 4.

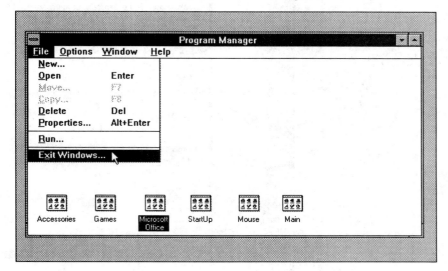

Figure 4

2. Mouse: Click Exit Windows.
   or Keys: Press **X**

3. Mouse: Click OK.
   or Keys: Press [ENTER]

GETTING HELP

The Help menu within the Program Manager provides assistance for the Program Manager and for most Windows concepts, commands, and terms. You access Help by choosing the Help command from the menu system. If you are in the process of executing a command, press [F1] for help.

➤ **To access Help, and then access the Help Contents:**

1. Make sure you are in Windows.

2. Mouse: Click Help.
   or Keys: Press [ALT] + **H**

3. Mouse: Click Contents.
   or Keys: Press **C**

   Your screen should look like Figure 5.

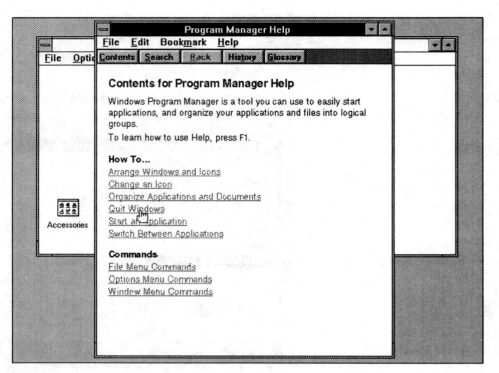

Figure 5

The Contents command, which displays the topics for the Program Manager Help, is a good place to begin exploring Help.

➤ **To get help quitting Windows:**

1. Mouse: Click Quit Windows under the How To heading.
   or Keys: Press `TAB` until you highlight Quit Windows, and then press `ENTER`

   You should see a description of how to exit Windows, as shown in Figure 6.

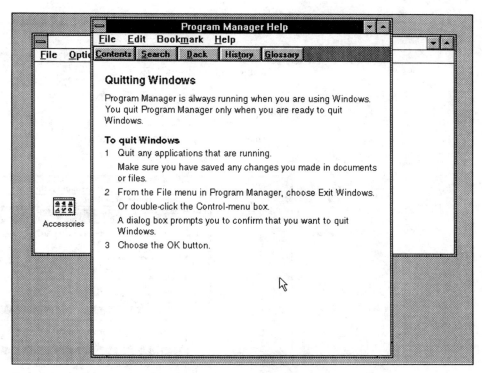

Figure 6

Figure 6 displays five buttons, common to all Help screens, that you can access by clicking or pressing `ALT` and the corresponding underlined letter. The Contents button displays the topics for the Program Manager Help, Search enables you to type keywords to look up Help information, Back takes you back to a previous Help screen, History lists the names of the Help screens that you have displayed, and Glossary provides a list of definitions for important words.

➤ **To go back to the previous Help screen:**

1. Mouse: Click the Back button.
   or Keys: Press `ALT` + **B**

   Your screen should display the Contents for the Program Manager Help screen. Notice that the Back button is dimmed to indicate that you cannot go back to any other Help screens; that is, this is the screen from which you started.

The Search button enables you to type in a keyword and then have Windows search for any information related to it.

➤ **To search for Help on starting an application:**

1. Mouse: Click the Search button.
   or Keys: Press [ALT] + **S**

2. Type **starting** and then press [ENTER]

   The search screen should display five topics that are found under *starting applications*, as shown in Figure 7.

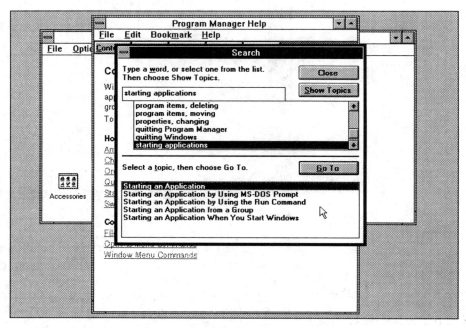

Figure 7

3. Mouse: Double-click Starting an Application from a Group.
   or Keys: Press [↓] until you highlight Starting an Application from a Group, and then press [ENTER]

   Your screen should display the Starting an Application from a Group Help screen.

➤ **To look up a word in the Glossary:**

1. Mouse: Click *group*
   or Keys: Press [TAB] until *group* is highlighted, and then press [ENTER]

2. Press [ESC] to return to the previous window.

   An alternative method for looking up the definition of a word is by clicking the Glossary button for a complete list of all of Windows' glossary items.

> **Tip**
> Now that you have seen how to access menu commands and screen buttons using either the mouse or the keyboard, you can use the method or combination of methods you prefer. From now on, the instructions will be stated in more general terms and will look like this:
> Choose Contents *or* Select Search
> The word *choose* refers to menu commands, and the word *select* refers to options (such as the Help buttons).

➤ To exit Help:

1. Choose Exit from the File Menu.

    If you access Help from within a software application, you will receive help on that particular application. The Help feature will work in the same fashion, but the command options and the Help screens will pertain to the application. In many applications, Help will be context-sensitive. For example, if you are in the process of saving a document in Microsoft Word and you press F1, you will get help on saving a document in Word and avoid searching through the Help screens to find the right screen.

USING THE PROGRAM MANAGER MENU

The *Program Manager* performs a pivotal role in the operation of Windows. It automatically opens every time you start Windows and remains in the background during your entire Windows session. When you are ready to quit Windows, you do so by closing the Program Manager. The Program Manager gives you a quick and easy way to start applications.

➤ To display the Program Manager:

1. If you have not done so already, start Windows.

    Figure 8 shows a typical Program Manager window. The names and the arrangement of the program group icons on your screen may be different.

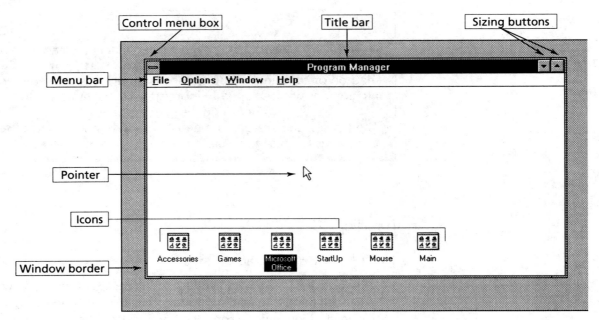

Figure 8

Each window has a *Control menu box* in its upper-left corner from which a drop-down menu appears that lists commands for controlling a window. With a mouse, you can use the *sizing buttons* to change the dimensions of the window quickly. The name of the application or document is displayed in the *title bar*. The *window border* defines the outside edge of the window.

Within Windows, you perform many operations by choosing menu options. The Program Manager's menus provide basic commands for managing windows and applications. For example, you can open, copy, and delete applications. You also can get help on the Program Manager and on other parts of Windows. When you select a menu from the menu bar, the menus that drop down follow three conventions that are common among most Windows menus: check marks, dimmed commands, and ellipses. A *check mark* next to a command name indicates that a command is active. Only optional commands that can be *toggled* (turned on and off) are displayed with check marks.

A *dimmed command* on a menu is not available at the current time. Some commands are available only during certain situations; when they are dimmed, they cannot be executed.

An *ellipsis*, a three-dot symbol (...) that follows certain commands, denotes that a dialog box will appear when the command is chosen. A *dialog box* is a rectangular box that either prompts the user to provide more information or provides information of its own, such as a warning or error message.

Using the Control Menu

When you select the Control menu box in the upper-left corner of a window, the Control menu drops down. If you are using a keyboard, the *Control menu* enables you to control window operations, such as moving, sizing, and closing windows. Mouse users perform these operations by clicking, double-clicking, or dragging windows. You can use the Control menu to close any window, including the Program Manager window. By closing the Program Manager window, you will exit Windows, in addition to closing the Program Manager.

➤ To close the active window:

1. Mouse: Click the Control menu box.
   or Keys: Press [ALT] and then press [SPACE]

   Be sure to click the Control menu box only once. Your screen should look like the one in Figure 9.

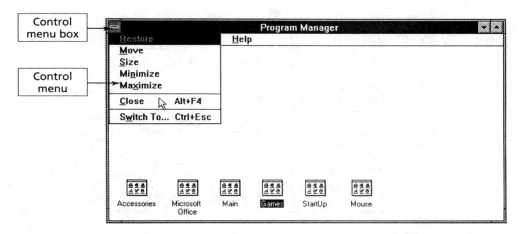

Figure 9

2. Choose Close.

   Notice that you get a dialog box to exit Windows.

3. Select Cancel.

   Most dialog boxes contain a Cancel button that enables you to cancel a command.

Moving a Window

Occasionally one window will hide another. A window can be moved by dragging its title bar or by using the Control menu.

➤ **To move the Program Manager window:**

1. Mouse: Place the pointer anywhere on the Program Manager title bar.
   or Keys: Press [ALT] + [SPACE]
2. Mouse: Click the title bar and hold down the mouse button.
   or Keys: Press **M**
3. Mouse: Drag the pointer a little to the right.
   or Keys: Press [→] a few times.
4. Mouse: Release the mouse button.
   or Keys: Press [ENTER]
5. Move the Program Manager window back to its original position.

Sizing a Window

Sizing a window requires a steady hand. You will move the pointer to the edge of the window until the pointer's shape changes, and then drag the edges.

> **Tip**
> Do not click the mouse in these operations until the pointer changes into the appropriate shape.
> ↔ Changes the width of a window
> ↕ Changes the height of a window
> ↘ Changes the height and width of a window simultaneously

➤ **To increase the height of a window:**

1. Mouse: Place the pointer on the upper border of the window until the pointer becomes double-pointed.
   or Keys: Press [ALT] + [SPACE] and then press **S**
2. Mouse: Drag the pointer upward a short distance, and then release the mouse button.
   or Keys: Press [↑] once to place the pointer on the upper border. Press [↑] a few times to move the upper border and then press [ENTER]

You can also change the height of a window by dragging the lower border up or down.

Introduction to Windows

➤ **To increase the width of a window:**

1. Mouse: Place the pointer on the right side of the window border until the pointer becomes double-pointed.
   or Keys: Press [ALT] + [SPACE] and then press **S**

2. Mouse: Drag the pointer a short distance to the right, and then let go of the mouse button.
   or Keys: Press [→] once to place the pointer on the right border.
   Press [→] a few times and then press [ENTER]

You can also change a window's width by dragging its left border left or right.

➤ **To simultaneously change the height and width of a window:**

1. Mouse: Place the pointer in the lower-right corner of the window until the pointer becomes diagonal and double-pointed.
   or Keys: Press [ALT] + [SPACE] and then press **S**
   Press [→] once, and then press [↓] once.

2. Mouse: Drag the pointer a short distance upward and to the left.
   or Keys: Press [↑] and [←] a few times and then press [ENTER]

Manipulating Windows

To concentrate all of your attention on one particular window, you can use the Windows Minimize and Maximize buttons shown in Figure 10. To *maximize* a window means to fill the entire screen with the window.

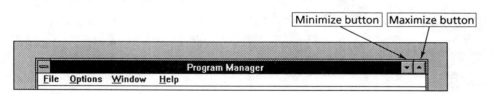

Figure 10

➤ **To maximize a window:**

1. Mouse: Click the Maximize button.
   or Keys: Press [ALT] + [SPACE] and then press **x**

The Program Manager window should fill the entire screen.

To *restore* a window means to bring it back to its previous size. The Restore button is shown in Figure 11.

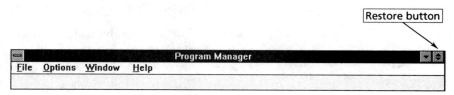

Figure 11

➤ **To restore a window after it has been maximized:**

1. Mouse: Click the Restore button.
   or Keys: Press ALT + SPACE and then press **R**

To *minimize* a window means to reduce it to an icon at the bottom of the screen. The application can be easily restored later to its former size by double-clicking the icon. An icon can be identified by its distinct shape or its name, which always appears below the icon.

➤ **To minimize and then restore the Program Manager:**

1. Mouse: Click the Minimize button.
   or Keys: Press ALT + SPACE and then press **N**

   The minimized Program Manager will be displayed as an icon.

2. Mouse: Double-click the Program Manager icon.
   or Keys: Press ALT + SPACE and then press **R**

Tip
If you are using the keyboard and have multiple application icons on the screen, you will need to press ALT + ESC to select the Program Manager icon before you can restore the Program Manager.

Working with Icons

Figure 12 shows Windows' three basic types of icons: application icons, group icons, and program-item icons.

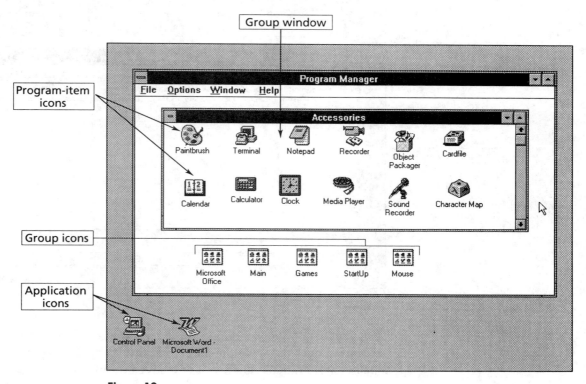

Figure 12

An *application icon* represents a program that has been minimized. In the Program Manager, *group icons* represent groups of programs. Group icons open into *group windows* filled with programs. In general, group icons look the same except for their labels.

A *program-item icon* is used to start an application. When you open a program-item icon, a window opens with the program inside. The Accessories group in Figure 12 contains program-item icons for programs such as the Clock, the Calculator, and the Calendar. If you were to open the Windows Applications group icon in Figure 12, you would see Word and Excel program-item icons in the group window. Word and Excel's program-item icons look the same as their application icons.

Starting a Program

One of the Program Manager's main roles is to start programs (lists of instructions). When you start a program, the Program Manager opens a window and places the program into it. Programs and their associated documents are contained in application and document windows.

An *application window* contains a running *application,* a program designed for a particular type of work. For example, the Program Manager runs in an application window as does a word processing program such as Microsoft Word. Figure 13 displays a Microsoft Word application window.

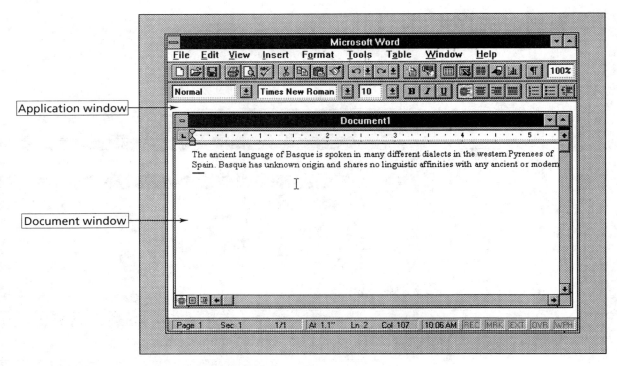

Figure 13

A *document window* is found inside of an application window and contains a *document,* such as a letter, memo, or report. If you are working on multiple documents simultaneously, you will have multiple document windows open.

The Program Manager uses group windows, such as the Accessories group window, which are similar to document windows because they reside within an application window.

➤ To open the Accessories group window:

1. Choose Options.

2. Mouse: Make sure Minimize On Use is *not* checked. If it is not checked, click the desktop. If it is checked, click Minimize On Use to toggle it on.
    or Keys: If Minimize On Use is *not* checked, press ESC twice; otherwise, press **M**

    When Minimize On Use is checked, the Program Manager will minimize itself every time that you open an application. In this introduction, we don't want that to happen.

3. Mouse: Double-click the Accessories group icon to open Accessories.
    or Keys: Press CTRL + F6 until the Accessories group icon is highlighted, and then press ENTER

The Accessories group includes utility programs that are provided as part of the Windows software package. For example, the *Calendar* serves as an electronic appointment book with an alarm to remind you of important appointments.

➤ To open the Calendar program:

1. Mouse: Double-click the Calendar program-item icon. If necessary, scroll through Accessories to find the Calendar.
    or Keys: Press the arrow keys until the Calendar is highlighted. Press ENTER

    Your screen should look like the one in Figure 14. Your Calendar may be positioned differently.

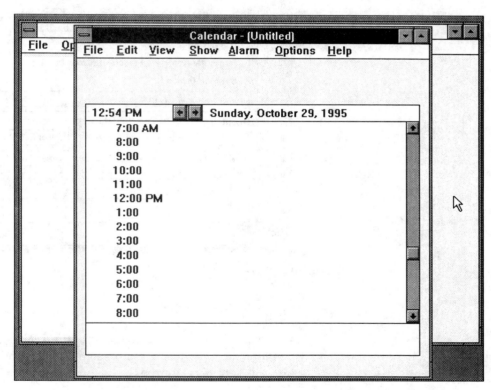

Figure 14

SETTING DIALOG BOX OPTIONS

Dialog boxes display information and prompt you to enter text. You can also adjust the settings of Windows options by using option buttons, command buttons, and check boxes. You move the cursor from one option to another by clicking the option or pressing TAB.

Option buttons appear in small groups of related options from which you can select only one item.

➤ **To set printer options:**

1. Choose Print Setup from the File menu.

    In the box labeled Orientation, you can choose one of two option buttons, Portrait or Landscape, as shown in Figure 15. A portrait orientation prints the document vertically on the paper; a landscape orientation prints horizontally.

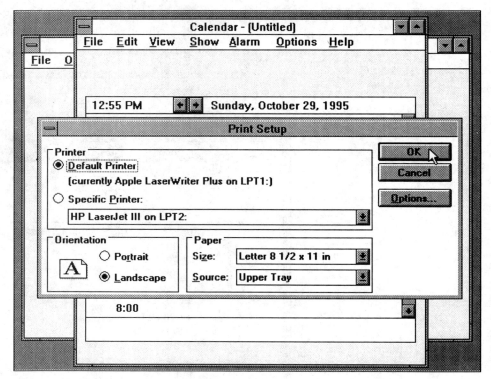

Figure 15

2. Select Landscape.

Command buttons are rectangular buttons labeled with an action. Figure 15 contains the two most common command buttons, OK and Cancel, and the Options command button.

➤ **To close a dialog box without saving any new settings:**

1. Select Cancel.

Exiting Programs

You can close most programs in Windows by choosing the Exit command from the File menu.

➤ **To exit the Calendar:**

1. Choose Exit from the File menu.

➤ **To restore the Program Manager and exit Windows:**

1. Restore the Program Manager.
2. Use one of the methods that you have learned to exit Windows.

    This concludes your introduction to Windows.

Introduction to WordPerfect 6 for Windows

The emphasis on teamwork, shared responsibility, and global awareness in today's organizations is creating a new ethic of communication and information sharing. To be an effective professional in today's world, you need to develop your interpersonal and communications skills, including your ability to organize information into readable, informative, useful *documents*.

Professional people communicate often. Their work requires them to meet with people, talk on the phone, and give oral presentations. They must also do a lot of writing. They write letters, memorandums, proposals, reports, manuals, posters, fliers, magazine articles, newsletters, questionnaires, forms, and many other types of documents. Increasingly, they write with a microcomputer using a *word processing* software package. Even Jessica Fletcher of "Murder, She Wrote" put her beloved typewriter aside in favour of a word processor.

Word processing software, such as WordPerfect 6 for Windows, enables you to create, edit, store, retrieve, and print documents. Documents are made up mostly of text—characters, words, and sentences. More recently, the term *word processing* has expanded to include the capability to integrate information from other sources and to include graphic art and other formatting capabilities to enhance the readability and usefulness of documents.

Word processing is a powerful information technology that gives you control over the content and the form of your writing. It is in your best interests to use this technology to improve the quality of all of your documents.

Getting Started

In this *BASIS* computer applications module for **WordPerfect 6 for Windows**, you will develop many of the skills outlined above. You will remember from the introductory section that within every topic in a *BASIS* module there are four sections: Topic Objectives, Computer Tutorial, Practice Exercises, and Competency Testing. *If you have not read the explanation of these four sections, please do so now before continuing further* (see **Introduction to the *BASIS* Modules**, pages vii to x).

First read the Topic Objectives, then start the computer tutorial. Take notes when necessary to fully understand the material. After you finish the computer tutorial sections indicated, work through the practice exercises. Finally, read the Competency Testing outline carefully since it summarizes the work you must have completed from the topic to qualify for the competency test at the end of the module.

Topic Objectives

As explained in the **Introduction to the *BASIS* Modules**, every major topic in a *BASIS* module begins with a list of topic objectives that outline for you:

- What you should learn from working through the topic.
- What you should expect to be able to demonstrate on the competency test.

In this **Introduction to WordPerfect 6 for Windows** topic, you will learn how to:

- Differentiate between basic and advanced word processing features (*Note:* Covered in Practice Exercises *only*).
- Start WordPerfect 6 for Windows.
- Describe the components of a WordPerfect 6 for Windows document window.
- Work with menus and dialog boxes using a mouse or the keyboard.
- Use the Power Bar and the Button Bar.
- Use the Help feature (*Note:* Covered in Practice Exercises *only*).
- Exit WordPerfect (*Note:* Covered in Practice Exercises *only*).

 # COMPUTER TUTORIAL

The sections from the WordPerfect tutorial listed below are to be covered for this **Introduction to WordPerfect 6 for Windows** topic.

- Select the *BASIS* **WordPerfect 6 Tutorial** in the manner indicated by your *BASIS* System Administrator[2] and/or your *BASIS* **User's Guide**.

- Work through:

    1.1   Starting Windows

    1.2   The WordPerfect Screen

    2.1   Using the Button Bar

    2.2   Using the Power Bar

- Note carefully the **Summary** and **Quiz** sections at the end of most tutorials.

NOTE

- Be sure to use the bookmark feature (by entering Name and Password).

    It will be very helpful to you, showing you what you have completed, and bringing you back at the right place when you resume work that you have interrupted.

    In addition, to qualify you to attempt the competency test at the end of this module, you must have covered the required work. This will be checked in part, by examining bookmark references on your disk.

- As you progress through tutorial exercises, explanations and instructions appear in a box identifying the Activity you are currently working through and the step you are on at the moment (e.g., "Activity 1.1 - Step 1 of 9").

    Sometimes the explanations and instructions are longer than the display box. When this occurs, use the vertical scroll bar on the right-hand side of the box to move down to see the last few lines.

- You may not be starting Windows in the way outlined in the tutorial. Be sure to start Windows in the manner indicated by your *BASIS* System Administrator and/or your *BASIS* **User's Guide**.

    Information on starting Windows from the DOS prompt is included in this *BASIS* module even though that may not be the case at your institution because that is the way you may start applications in many other environments (future jobs, for example).

    Additionally, Step 7 of Activity 1.1 describes starting Windows and WordPerfect in one step. This may not be possible at your institution and/or in your working environment.

---

[2] The term System Administrator is used throughout to designate the person responsible for management of the *BASIS* system where you are using it. Your institution may refer to this person in another way.

- Icons may not appear in your Windows WordPerfect window exactly as portrayed in the tutorial (e.g. some may be missing). Do not be concerned.

Practice Exercises

If this is the first BASIS *module you have used, be sure you have read through the introductory section at the beginning of this book for an explanation of the way the module is organized.*

In all Practice Exercises in this module (*except* this one), you must print a "topic directory listing" showing files on your data diskette after completing *all* Practice Exercises work (including Review Exercises). Do this in the manner indicated by your *BASIS* System Administrator and/or your *BASIS* **User's Guide**.

The practice exercise activities for the **Introduction to WordPerfect 6 for Windows** topic are:

- Read pages 5 to 20, which follow. Make notes in the margins and/or highlight material as you go where you find it necessary to do so to fully understand the material covered. The **Summary** and **Key Terms and Operations** sections are especially helpful. (There are no files to be saved in this practice exercises section.)

- Do **Multiple Choice** exercises on page 20.

NOTE

- In order to use WordPerfect 6 for Windows, you must be running Windows. If you are new to Windows, be sure to read **Introduction to Windows** (pp. xi to xxix). Additionally, **Activity 1.1** provides an orientation to Windows.

- As previously indicated in the NOTE with the Computer Tutorial, you may not be starting Windows in the way indicated in the tutorial and the WordPerfect icons that appear in your WordPerfect window once you start Windows may not exactly match those portrayed in the tutorial. Be sure to start Windows in the manner indicated by your *BASIS* System Administrator and/or your *BASIS* **User's Guide**.

- Since WordPerfect may be set up in a number of different ways, your screen may not look exactly like Figure 0.2 on page 8. Here are reasons why this may be the case, and the steps you can take to make your screens resemble those in this text:

    - Your menu bar may not be displayed. To turn it on, press [ALT] - [V] (that is, press and hold [ALT] and then press [V]), then select Hide Bars.
    - Your Button Bar may not be displayed. To turn it on, pull down the View menu (either by pressing View from the menu bar *or* by pressing [ALT] - [V]), then select Button Bar (highlight Button Bar by dragging your mouse down *or* by using [↓]), then press [ENTER].

- Your Power and/or Status Bars may not be displayed. Turn them on using the same method as for turning on the Button Bar, described immediately above.

- While you do not actually create any files in these practice exercises, and you may be understandably anxious to move ahead to project work where you feel you are actually "doing something" (creating a document), *this introductory topic is especially important*: it outlines all of the basic methods for "moving around" in WordPerfect 6 for Windows and answers many "how do I?" kinds of questions, which will occur to you in later topics if you fail to pay close attention here. Mastering the Help utility, and knowing how to access the menu bar, and use the Button, Power, and Status bars build the foundation upon which the following topics in the module are based.

    After you have finished the practice exercises, be sure to scan the Summary and Key Terms and Operations sections, as suggested above. If you come across terms or concepts you don't recognize, it's a good idea to do a quick review.

Using a Word Processor

Word processing is the most widely used application for microcomputers. A word processing software package is an easy-to-use yet powerful tool for typing, revising, enhancing, and printing text as well as storing and retrieving documents on disk.

All word processors have certain basic features and capabilities in common. Text is displayed on the computer monitor as you type. One character can be typed at the *insertion point,* which is a blinking vertical line that moves from left to right as you type characters on each line on the screen. You can move the insertion point anywhere in the document to insert new text or make corrections. The *word wrap* feature automatically moves the word you've just typed and advances the insertion point to the beginning of the next line when the text on the previous line approaches the right margin. You can type documents of any length.

The *scrolling* feature moves text outside the screen as you type lines of text. You can also scroll forward and backward to find a particular location in a document. You can automatically search the document for specific text and replace it with other text with *search and replace* operations. *Block operations* enable you to copy, move, or delete any selected text. You can *format* a document by changing margins, tab settings, indentations, and justification.

Many document-enhancing capabilities are available, such as changing the font and size of text; changing the appearance of text by boldfacing, underlining, or italicizing characters; using superscripts and subscripts; specifying where page numbers should be printed; and including headers, footers, footnotes, and endnotes. *File operations* enable you to save documents to disk and retrieve them for later revision or printing.

In addition to these basic features, many word processing software products, including WordPerfect 6 for Windows, provide more advanced yet easy-to-use features that increase your writing productivity. Some of the advanced features discussed in this module and what they do are listed in Table 0.1.

Table 0.1

FEATURE	FUNCTION
Spell checking	Verifies the spelling of a word, a block of text, or the entire document.
Thesaurus	Looks up synonyms or antonyms of words.
Desktop publishing	Incorporates graphic art, line drawings, tables, and multiple columns into your text to create high-quality, eye-catching documents.
Merging	Creates custom documents by combining data from other documents and other computer sources into one document.

Using WordPerfect 6 for Windows

WordPerfect 6 for Windows is a full-featured word processing software package that also takes advantage of the graphical user interface (GUI, pronounced "goo-ee") provided by Microsoft Windows. The Windows environment lets you easily access word processing features using a mouse, menus, dialog boxes, and buttons displayed on the screen, or ***document window.***

You can type text in the document window and then scroll through the document using a scroll bar. You can insert, delete, and correct text, and you can easily move, copy, or delete blocks of text using a mouse. With easy-to-use dialog boxes, you can automatically search for and replace a specific word or phrase. You can easily set margins and tabs on a ruler displayed in the document window. You can insert graphics images into the document. You can see the formatting and enhancements to the document on the screen, which makes it easy to determine what revisions are necessary. With as many as nine document windows open at one time, you can easily copy and move text between documents. It is also easy to save, retrieve, and print documents.

The Help feature provides information about all the features of WordPerfect 6 for Windows. You can use Help whenever you are working on a document. The Help feature is discussed in a separate section later in this overview.

Starting WordPerfect 6 for Windows

The following numbered steps assume that WordPerfect 6 for Windows is installed in the WPWIN60 directory on the hard disk and that the WordPerfect program files are organized as a group in Windows. The group consists of icons that represent WordPerfect, Speller, Thesaurus, and other program files. To start WordPerfect 6 for Windows, you start the Windows program, open the WordPerfect group window, and locate the WordPerfect application icon, as shown in Figure 0.1. (You may not see all the icons shown in Figure 0.1, depending on how WordPerfect was installed on your computer.)

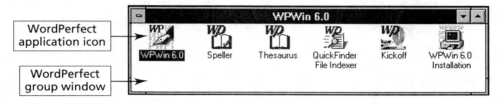

Figure 0.1

> **Tip**
> Throughout this module, when a numbered step asks you to select a button or icon, you will see the button or icon displayed next to that step to introduce it to you.

➤ To start WordPerfect 6 for Windows:

1. Start Windows.

2. Double-click the WordPerfect (WPWIN6.0) group icon, if displayed on the screen.

    If the WordPerfect group window is already open, skip to the next step.

3. Double-click the WordPerfect (WPWIN6.0) application icon.

    A copyright screen is displayed for a few seconds, and then a WordPerfect document window opens as shown in Figure 0.2.

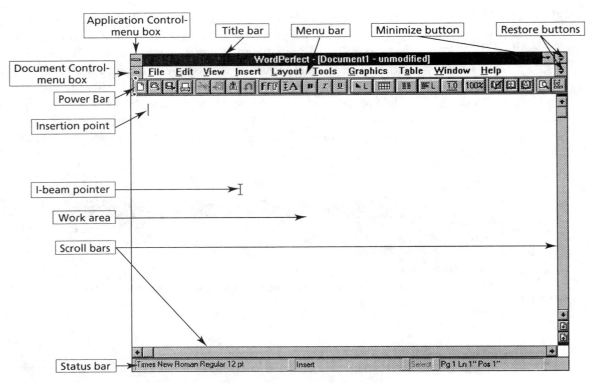

Figure 0.2

USING THE DOCUMENT WINDOW

The WordPerfect 6 for Windows document window, shown in Figure 0.2, contains several components. The blank portion of the screen is the *work area,* where a document is displayed while you type. The insertion point is displayed as a flashing vertical line, initially at the upper-left corner of the work area, and indicates where text will appear as you type. Surrounding three sides of the work area are the various controls and displays that enable you to use WordPerfect's features, either with a mouse or the keyboard. You use the mouse to point to items on the screen. When the pointer is positioned in the work area, it has the shape of a capital *I* and is called the *I-beam pointer.* It changes to a large arrow when you point to areas outside of the work area.

The *title bar* across the top of the screen indicates both the application you are working in, WordPerfect, and the name of the document you are working on. The title Document1 will be replaced by the name you give the document when you save it to disk. There are also three Windows control boxes on the title bar. The *application Control-menu box* in the upper-left corner lets you either exit WordPerfect or minimize the WordPerfect application and then switch to another application. At the right end of the title bar are a *Minimize button* (a single down arrow) and a *Maximize button* (a single up arrow) or a *Restore button* (a double arrow). The Minimize button reduces the WordPerfect application to an icon. The Maximize button changes the size of the WordPerfect window, filling the entire screen. The Restore button reduces the WordPerfect window size. You will learn more about how to use these control boxes later in this overview.

The second horizontal bar from the top of the screen is the *menu bar*. The menu bar contains the names of the ten main WordPerfect for Windows menus. From each of these menus you will choose the specific commands that you will need to work with your document. The File menu contains commands you can use to manipulate documents as a whole, such as Save, Retrieve, and Print. The Edit menu has commands for changing and correcting text in a document. The View menu lets you change the way the document appears on the screen. The Insert menu lets you place a date, footnotes, and special characters into the document. The Layout menu modifies the appearance of lines, paragraphs, and pages in the document. The Tools menu contains the spell checker, thesaurus, and other commands for merging documents. The Graphics menu lets you create your own drawings and incorporate them and other clip art into a document. You use the Table menu to organize information into a column-and-row format. The Window menu lets you arrange and move among a maximum of nine document windows on the screen. The Help menu provides a comprehensive memory aid on all the features of WordPerfect 6 for Windows. You will learn how to use Help later in this overview. You will learn how to use the other menus in Projects 1 through 8.

Two Windows control boxes are located on the menu bar. The *document Control-menu box* at the leftmost edge of the menu bar lets you either exit the document or minimize the document window and then switch to another document. At the right end of the menu bar is a Restore button (a double arrow) to reduce the size of the document window.

The row of buttons just below the menu bar is the *Power Bar,* which lets you quickly perform frequently used text editing and layout commands without having to go through the various menus. You can choose to display or not display the Power Bar by choosing Power Bar from the View menu. You can also use the View menu to display a *Button Bar* and a *Ruler Bar,* not shown in Figure 0.2. The Button Bar lets you quickly select virtually any WordPerfect command. You can use the Ruler Bar to change the margins in a document easily. You will learn how to use the Ruler Bar in Project 3.

A vertical *scroll bar,* on the right side of the screen, and a horizontal scroll bar, on the bottom of the screen are used to move through a document to bring the desired portion of the document into view in the work area. You can decide to display or not display the scroll bars by choosing them from the View menu. You will learn more about how to use scroll bars in Project 1.

The last component of the document window is the *status bar,* located across the bottom of the screen below the horizontal scroll bar. The location of the insertion point is displayed as coordinates at the right end of the status bar. The three values indicate the page in the document, the line from the top of the page, and the position on the line from the left edge of the page. Other information and messages are displayed at the left end and middle of the status bar when WordPerfect is performing certain functions or tasks.

WordPerfect 6 for Windows

Using WordPerfect Commands

There are three ways to access WordPerfect commands: by using the mouse to access commands from the menu bar and menus, by using available buttons on the Power Bar or Button Bar to make selections, and by using keystroke combinations to bypass one or more menu selections. You may need to provide additional information in a dialog box in any of the three methods.

CHOOSING MENU OPTIONS USING THE MOUSE

WordPerfect's menu bar contains one-word menu names. Choosing an option on the menu bar displays a *pull-down menu*, which displays additional options. When you choose an option that has a triangle symbol at the right side, another menu is displayed with still more options. An example of a pull-down menu is shown in Figure 0.3. When you choose an option that has three dots (called ellipses) following its name, you will see a *dialog box* in which you type additional information. Dialog boxes are discussed later in this overview. An option that can be turned on and off is called a *toggle*; an option is turned on when a check mark is displayed on the left side of the option.

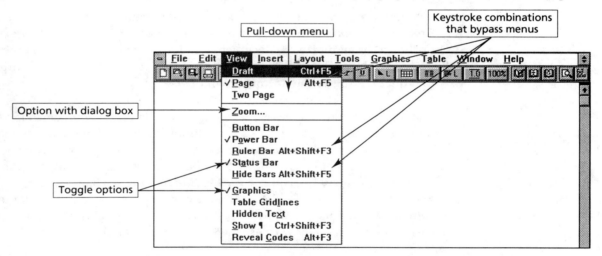

Figure 0.3

You choose a menu option with the mouse by moving the pointer to the menu bar, pointing to a specific menu option, and then pressing and releasing (clicking) the left mouse button. When the menu is displayed, you point to the desired option to select it. You can press and hold down the left mouse button when the pointer is on an option to display a short description of the option on the title bar. Once you release the button, the option is executed; if you don't want to execute the option, move the mouse pointer off the menu before releasing the mouse button.

➤ **To use a mouse for menu selections:**

1. Click View on the menu bar.
2. Click Ruler Bar to display the Ruler Bar across the top of the document window.

3. Click View on the menu bar.
4. Click Ruler Bar to turn off the display of the Ruler Bar.

USING THE KEYBOARD AND KEYSTROKE COMBINATIONS

Another method of choosing commands is to use the keyboard to navigate through the menu structure and bypass the use of the mouse. You press [ALT] to activate the menu bar, and then you either type the underlined character of the menu option you want or press [→] or [←] to highlight the desired option and press [ENTER]. The menu is displayed, and then you choose the desired option by either typing the underlined character or using [↑] or [↓] to highlight the option and press [ENTER].

Many menu options have keystroke combinations displayed on the right side of the pull-down menu, as shown in Figure 0.3. Using these keystroke combinations, you can bypass many of the menus. For example, if you want to center text on a line, you can press [CTRL] +**E** instead of choosing Layout from the menu bar and then choosing Justification and Center from the pull-down menus. As you use WordPerfect 6 for Windows over time, you will be able to remember the keystroke combinations that are the most useful to you.

➤ To choose commands using keyboard and keystroke combinations:

1. Press [ALT] +**V** to access the View menu.
2. Type **R** to toggle the Ruler Bar on or off.
3. Press [ALT] + [SPACE] + [F3] to toggle the Ruler Bar on or off.

CANCELLING AND UNDOING COMMANDS

As you are invoking a command using any of the previously mentioned methods, you may realize that this is not what you really want to do. It is easy to cancel a partially executed command. If you have chosen a menu item and a menu is displayed, you can press [ESC] or click anywhere off the menu bar. (You may have to press [ESC] more than once.) If a dialog box is displayed, you can click the Close or Cancel button.

After you have invoked a command, you might change your mind and want to reverse the change you just made. It is easy to change the effects of the most recent command that you executed by choosing Undo from the Edit menu or by pressing [CTRL] +**Z**. However, not all operations can be undone.

USING THE POWER BAR AND THE BUTTON BAR

Another way to choose a command is to select the appropriate button on the Power Bar or the Button Bar. Each button represents a menu selection that is executed when you select the button, similar to what happens when you use a keyboard combination. Buttons are displayed as graphic icons, some with text to remind you of the button's function. The Power Bar buttons represent the most frequently used text editing and text layout commands. You can select 1 of 12 predefined sets of buttons to be displayed on the Button Bar. You can add, delete, and move buttons to customize the Power Bar and the Button Bar for your convenience, but you will not be customizing them in this module. You can toggle the Power Bar and the Button Bar on and off the document window. The Power Bar is always displayed beneath the menu bar, but the Button Bar is designed as a window and can be repositioned by dragging.

USING DIALOG BOXES

You will frequently need to use a dialog box to provide additional information to complete a command sequence. For example, Figure 0.4 shows the dialog box displayed after you choose Open from the File menu.

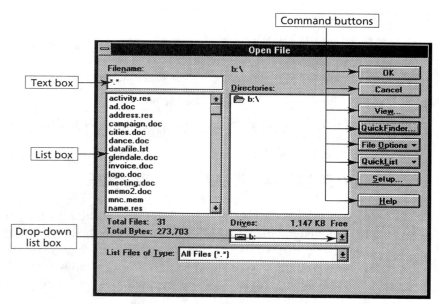

Figure 0.4

The dialog box usually appears in the center of the screen. You provide information by using various elements in the dialog box. A ***text box*** is used to enter and edit text settings, usually a file name. A ***list box*** displays an alphabetized list of choices. Two or more list boxes may be displayed, depending on the particular dialog box. WordPerfect fills in the text box with choices you highlight in the list boxes. A ***drop-down list box,*** which also provides a list of choices, looks like a button with a down arrow or a double arrow at the right side. When you select the button, a list of choices drops down just below the list box. A *check box* is a square box next to an item that is used to toggle an option on or off. An X is displayed in the box when you select that option. A *radio button* is a circle next to an item in a group of related but mutually exclusive items. You can choose only one item in the group. A black dot appears in the center when you select the option. A *preview window* shows how changes you are making will look in the document, as shown in Figure 0.5.

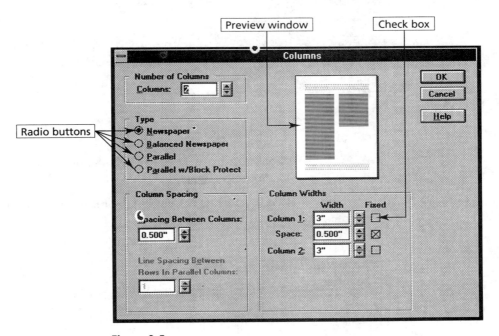

Figure 0.5

Some dialog boxes display choices as icons. You select the desired icon by double-clicking. Another dialog box is then displayed.

After you have entered information using the various text boxes and buttons in the dialog box, you must select the appropriate *command button* to continue or cancel the command sequence. There are usually at least two command buttons, labeled OK and Cancel, located at the right side of the dialog box. Most dialog boxes have additional command buttons, such as Print, Select, and Close. A command button with ellipses displays another dialog box. Most dialog boxes also have a Help button you can use to view information about the features and options of that dialog box.

➤ **To enter specifications using an icon, a list box, and command buttons:**

1. Mouse: Click File on the menu bar.
   or Keys: Press `ALT` + **F**

2. Mouse: Click Preferences.
   or Keys: Type **E**

The Preferences dialog box is displayed on the screen as shown in Figure 0.6.

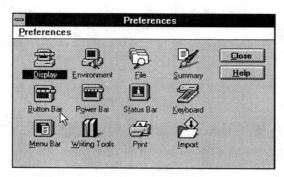

Figure 0.6

3. Mouse: Double-click the Button Bar icon.
   or Keys: Press the arrow keys to select the Button Bar icon text, and then press [ENTER]

Verify that your screen is displaying the Button Bar Preferences dialog box, as shown in Figure 0.7.

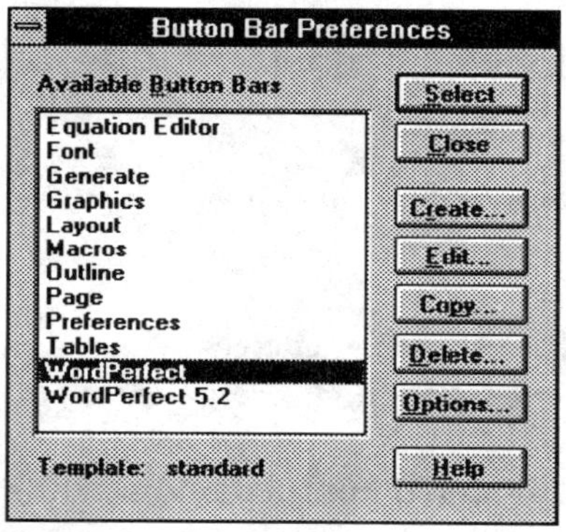

Figure 0.7

4. Mouse: Click Layout in the list box.
   or Keys: Press [↑] or [↓] to move up or down the list until Layout is highlighted.

Layout is the name of one of the twelve sets of buttons available for your use on the Button Bar. The Button Bar displays the currently selected set.

5. Mouse: Click Select.
   or Keys: Press [TAB] until a dotted line is displayed around the text on the Select command button, and then press [ENTER]

The Button Bar Preferences dialog box disappears from the screen, and both the selected Button Bar and the Preferences dialog box remain displayed.

Introduction to WordPerfect 6 for Windows

6. Mouse: Click Close.
   or Keys: Press `TAB` until a dotted line is displayed around the text on the Close command button, and then press `ENTER`

The Preferences dialog box disappears from the screen.

The Button Bar remains displayed on the screen. You can quickly remove the Button Bar by clicking the View Button Bar button on the far right end of the Power Bar.

Getting Online Help

WordPerfect for Windows provides a comprehensive Help tool that you can use in a variety of ways to view information about any feature in the WordPerfect application. This online information can be *context-sensitive Help*, which provides information about whatever feature you are currently using on the document window. You can also use the Help menu to view information about how to do a particular word processing task, descriptions or definitions of particular word processing topics or terms, a graphic presentation of the keyboard layout and keystroke combinations, or even help using the Help feature.

Help information is displayed in a window titled WordPerfect Help. The WordPerfect Help window has a Button Bar that provides quick access to information. Some words and phrases in the Help window are *jump terms*, which are highlighted with a solid underline, or *pop-up terms*, which are highlighted with a dotted underline. You can jump to more information on related topics by selecting a jump term. You can see the definition or information about a pop-up term by selecting the pop-up term. The pointer changes to a hand icon when you point to a jump term or a pop-up term. Figure 0.8 shows the general information Help window.

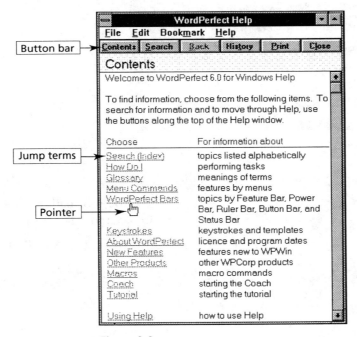

Figure 0.8

In the following steps, you will use the Help feature to find more information about on-screen Help.

➤ To display general information about online Help:

1. Move the pointer anywhere in the work area of the document window.

2. Press [F1]

   The Contents window of Help is displayed on the screen as shown in Figure 0.8.

3. Mouse: Click the jump term *Using Help.*
   or Keys: Press [TAB] to select the jump term *Using Help,* and then press [ENTER]

   The window titled Using Help is displayed on the screen as shown in Figure 0.9.

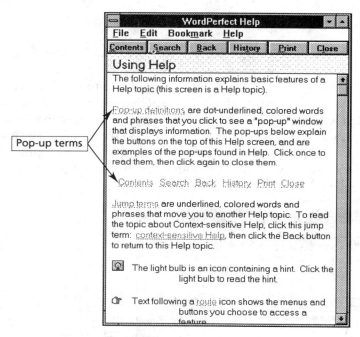

Figure 0.9

4. Select each pop-up and jump term in the work area of the window.

   You will get a good feel for the kinds of information available and how to navigate in Help by reading the information displayed.

5. Mouse: Click Close on the Button Bar in the WordPerfect Help window.
   or Keys: Press [ALT] + [F4]

   The Help window disappears from the screen.

CONTEXT-SENSITIVE HELP

You can view context-sensitive Help any time by pressing the Help key, `F1`, when the pointer is on a selected item, such as a menu command or a dialog box. Another way to view context-sensitive Help is by pressing `SHFT` + `F1`. Then you can use the pointer, which will be displayed as a question mark, to select any feature on the document window and view information on that item.

➤ **To display information about the File menu using `F1` :**

1. Mouse: Click File on the menu bar and press but do not release the mouse button.
   or Keys: Press `ALT` and then press `→`
2. Press `F1`
   The File menu Help screen is displayed.
3. Select the jump terms that are of interest to you.
4. Mouse: Click Close on the Button Bar in the WordPerfect Help window to exit Help.
   or Keys: Press `ALT` + `F4`

➤ **To display information about the document window using the question-mark pointer:**

1. Keys: Press `SHFT` + `F1`
   The pointer is displayed with a question mark next to it.
2. Point to View on the menu bar and click.
   The View menu WordPerfect Help window is displayed.
3. Mouse: Click Close on the Button Bar in the WordPerfect Help window to exit Help.
   or Keys: Press `ALT` + `F4`

WORDPERFECT HELP FEATURES

WordPerfect Help provides a variety of ways to make it easy to find the information you are looking for. You use the Button Bar at the top of the WordPerfect Help window to focus on a desired category of information. If you want to find out how to perform a word processing task, such as saving a document to disk, you can click the Contents button and then select the *How Do I* jump term. If you want in-depth information about a particular topic, you can use the Search button. If you read an unfamiliar term or phrase in a Help window, you can use the *Glossary* jump term in the Contents window. If you want to reread information about a topic you have already looked up, you can use either the Back button or the History button.

In the following steps, you will use Help to learn more about scroll bars.

➤ To search for information in Help:

1. Mouse: Click Help on the menu bar.
   or Keys: Press `ALT`+**H**

2. Mouse: Click Contents.
   or Keys: Type **C**

   The Contents window is displayed.

3. Mouse: Click the *Glossary* jump term.
   or Keys: Press `TAB` until the *Glossary* jump term is highlighted and then press `ENTER`

   The Glossary window is displayed.

4. Mouse: Click the button labeled S.
   or Keys: Press `TAB` to select the button labeled S, and then press `ENTER`

5. Mouse: Click the scroll bar pop-up term.
   or Keys: Press `TAB` to select the pop-up term, and then press `ENTER`

   Your screen will look similar to Figure 0.10.

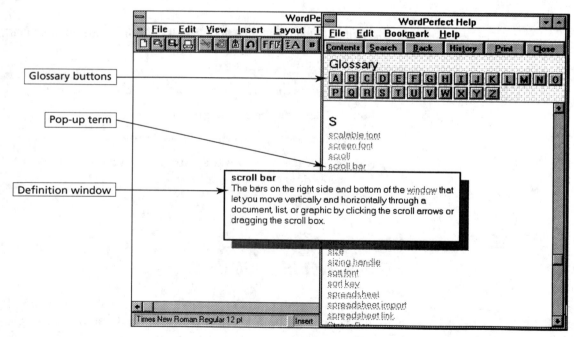

Figure 0.10

You use the other WordPerfect Help window buttons to search for information in a similar manner.

6. Click anywhere in the window to close the scroll bar definition window.

7. Mouse: Click Close on the Button Bar in the WordPerfect Help window to exit Help.
   or Keys: Press `ALT` + `F4`

Exiting WordPerfect 6 for Windows

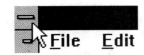

It is important to exit WordPerfect when you are finished using the application. You can close any Windows application, including WordPerfect for Windows, by choosing Close from the application Control-menu box.

You can also exit WordPerfect for Windows by choosing Exit from the File menu.

➤ **To exit WordPerfect for Windows using the File menu:**

1. Mouse: Click File on the menu bar.
   or Keys: Press `ALT` + **F**
2. Mouse: Click Exit.
   or Keys: Type **x**

You used some of the WordPerfect 6 for Windows features in this overview, but you did not create or edit a document. Project 1 covers these topics, as well as how to save and then exit a WordPerfect document.

This concludes this overview. You can either exit WordPerfect for Windows or go on to review the Summary and work the Study Questions.

Summary

- WordPerfect for Windows is a word processing software package that you can use to write high-quality documents.
- You type your work in a document window.
- A document window includes the following components: a title bar, a menu bar, a Power Bar, a Button Bar, a Ruler Bar, the work area, vertical and horizontal scroll bars, and a status bar.
- To invoke commands, you can choose menu options using a mouse or the keyboard, or you can use available command buttons or keystroke combinations.
- A dialog box is displayed when you need to provide additional information to complete a command sequence. You enter text or select options from list boxes, drop-down list boxes, radio buttons, and check boxes. You click a command button to finally carry out the action.
- The Help feature provides definitions and descriptions of menus, commands, procedures, and concepts.

Key Terms and Operations

Key Terms

application Control-menu box	I-beam pointer	scrolling
block operation	insertion point	search and replace
Button Bar	jump term	status bar
check box	list box	text box
command button	Maximize button	title bar
context-sensitive Help	menu bar	toggle
dialog box	Minimize button	word processing
document	pop-up term	word wrap
document Control-menu box	Power Bar	work area
document window	preview window	**Operations**
drop-down list box	pull-down menu	Exit
file operation	radio button	File
format	Restore button	Help
	Ruler Bar	View
	scroll bar	

Study Questions

MULTIPLE CHOICE

1. What would a word processing software package have as an advanced feature or capability?
   a. word wrap
   b. text scrolling
   c. different ways to format the text
   d. ability to include graphics into the document
   e. file operations

2. The portion of the document window into which you actually type the text of your document is called the:
   a. title bar.
   b. menu bar.
   c. Ruler Bar.
   d. work area.
   e. status bar.

3. You can execute a command using:
   a. the menu bar or the status bar.
   b. the menu bar or keystroke combinations.
   c. the Button Bar or the scroll bar.
   d. the Minimize and Maximize buttons.
   e. the title bar.

4. What do you click to carry out the actions specified in a dialog box?
   a. radio button
   b. command button
   c. check box
   d. drop-down list box
   e. arrow

5. You can find the definition of *layout* in:
   a. the status line.
   b. the scroll bar.
   c. the Help Glossary.
   d. the View menu.
   e. a dialog box.

SHORT ANSWER

1. Describe the components of a document window.
2. Describe the different ways to execute a command in WordPerfect for Windows. When do you use a dialog box?
3. Discuss the differences between context-sensitive Help and general Help.
4. For what kinds of questions would you use the Glossary? the Index? How do you access the various Help features?

COMPETENCY TESTING

- Review the Topic Objectives to ensure you have mastered all skills listed.
- Check off your completed Multiple Choice exercises in the manner outlined in your *BASIS* **User's Guide** ("Check Off of Work").
- Examine the **Multiple Choice Correct Answer Sheet** for this topic and compare your answers against the correct ones. Refer to your *BASIS* **User's Guide** ("Correct Answer Sheets") for the correct procedure, if you are uncertain.

Creating a Document

Topic Objectives

After completing this topic, you should be able to:

- Lay out the design of a WordPerfect document (*Note:* Covered in Practice Exercises *only*).
- Enter text into a document.
- Move the insertion point around in a document.
- Correct simple mistakes.
- Name a document.
- Save a document to disk.
- Preview a document (*Note:* Covered in Practice Exercises *only*).
- Print a document.
- Exit a document.

Computer Tutorial

- Work through:
2.3	Opening and Saving Files
3.1	Moving Around a Document
3.2	Selecting and Editing Text
4.1	Printing a Document

Practice Exercises

- Read and complete all **Project 1 work** outlined on pages 23 to 36:
    - Take special note of the **Summary** and **Key Terms and Operations** sections.
    - Make sure to save the file **SEQUOIA.LTR** as indicated on pages 31 and 35.
- Do **Multiple Choice** exercises on pages 37 and 38.

- Do all **Review Exercises** on pages 38 and 39, making sure to save the file **SHERMAN.DOC**.
- Do the required **Topic Directory Listing (TDL)**.

NOTE
- As you know from **Activity 2.2** in the computer tutorial, a variety of different *fonts* are available in WordPerfect. Additionally, any given font selected can be changed to a number of different sizes. You will learn more about this in the **Enhancing a Document** topic.

When you start doing the project work in this topic, you may notice that *what is on your screen does not match the figures in this book.* If this is the case, it is probably because the default font/size setting for WordPerfect 6 for Windows where you are using it is different from that used to make up the examples in the figures. If you would like to make your screen (and document) resemble the figures in this book, try setting your font to Courier New (TT) or Courier and the size to 12 points. Do this before you start, either by pressing the font button on the Power Bar or by selecting Font from the Layout pull-down menu.

PROJECT 1: CREATING A DOCUMENT

Case Study: Writing a Job Application Letter

You can think of many situations in which you need to communicate your thoughts on paper to another person. Many of these messages are relatively short, such as a letter to your mom or a short essay in your English class. Some messages are much longer, such as a term paper or a research project. Whatever the message length, you need to organize your word processing task using a three-step method. First, you need to identify the purpose of the message: to inform or inquire, to persuade, or to entertain. Second, you need to keep in mind the intended reader and organize the message in your own mind in a way that will be meaningful and makes sense to the person receiving the message. Third, you must actually produce the document.

For this first project, imagine you are applying for a job and want to schedule an interview with an employer. You need to write a short letter to the employer.

DESIGNING THE SOLUTION

You should always lay out the design of the document you want to write. Think of the document as a rectangle in which you lay out the information from left to right, line by line, down the page. You need to decide on the components of the document and how to arrange them on the page. For a letter, these parts include the date; the sender's address information; the address of the person being sent the letter; a salutation line; the opening, middle, and ending paragraphs; and the signature lines. You need to design your document well so that the intended reader will be able to read and understand it easily. This module includes design guidelines for different types of documents.

Now you are ready to type the document. You will actually do four things: first, you will type the text; second, you will correct any mistakes and make any desired revisions; third, you will save the document; and fourth, you will print the document. In this project, you will be working with the document shown in Figure 1.1.

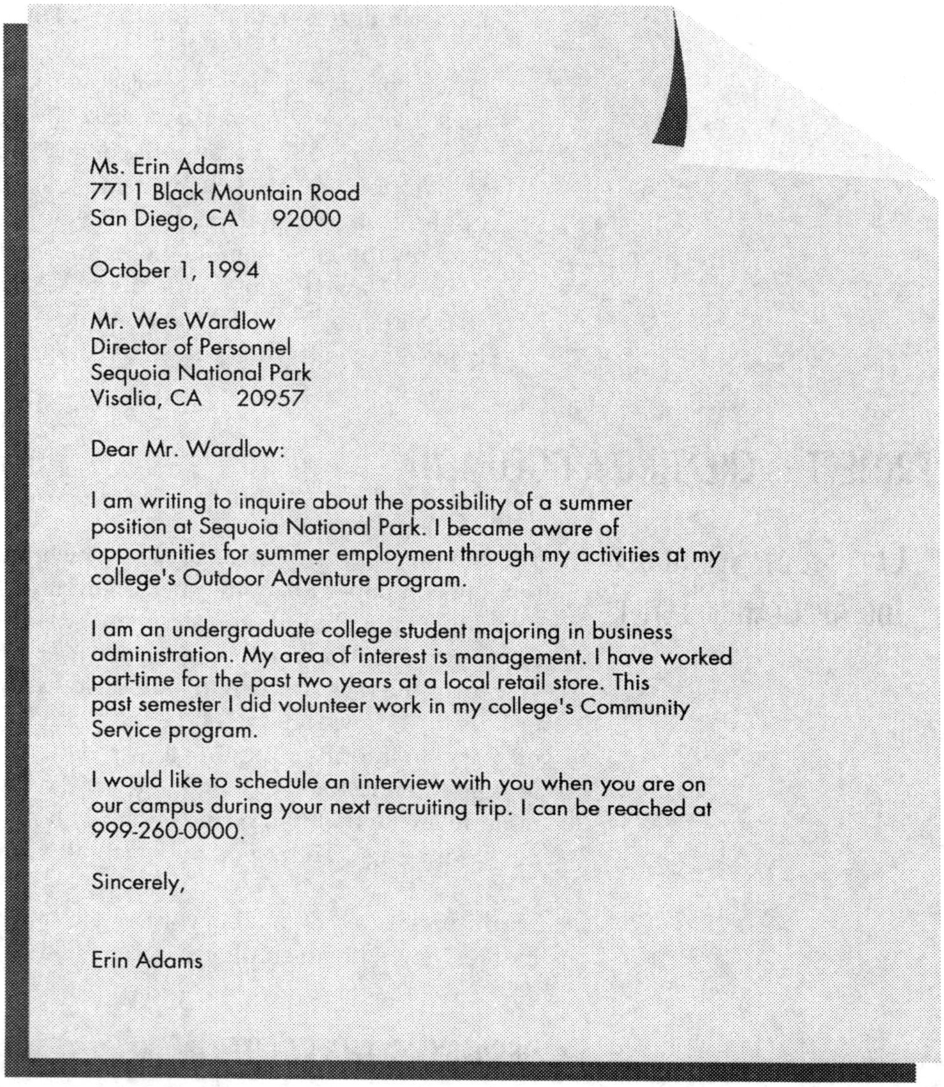

Ms. Erin Adams
7711 Black Mountain Road
San Diego, CA   92000

October 1, 1994

Mr. Wes Wardlow
Director of Personnel
Sequoia National Park
Visalia, CA   20957

Dear Mr. Wardlow:

I am writing to inquire about the possibility of a summer position at Sequoia National Park. I became aware of opportunities for summer employment through my activities at my college's Outdoor Adventure program.

I am an undergraduate college student majoring in business administration. My area of interest is management. I have worked part-time for the past two years at a local retail store. This past semester I did volunteer work in my college's Community Service program.

I would like to schedule an interview with you when you are on our campus during your next recruiting trip. I can be reached at 999-260-0000.

Sincerely,

Erin Adams

Figure 1.1

ENTERING TEXT

Typing text using WordPerfect is similar to using a typewriter, with a few exceptions. A single character is entered at the insertion point, the short vertical line that shows the current location in the document at which typed text will appear. Try to type without worrying about making mistakes, because it is easy to make corrections later. A major difference between typing on a typewriter and in a word processing program is that, with word processing, you type continually without pressing [ENTER] at the end of each line. A feature called word wrap automatically advances the insertion point to the beginning of the next line when a line of text is full. You press [ENTER] at the end of a *paragraph,* even if the paragraph is only a single line of text, or to add a blank line to the document. Whenever you press [ENTER], the insertion point advances to the beginning of the next line.

Start WordPerfect to begin this project. A blank document window is opened automatically, and you can begin typing.

➤ To enter single lines of text and blank lines:

1. Type **Ms. Erin Adams** and press [ENTER]
2. Type **7711 Black Mountain Road** and press [ENTER]
3. Type **San Diego, CA 92000** and press [ENTER]
4. Press [ENTER] to insert a blank line.
5. Type **October 1, 1994** and press [ENTER] twice.
6. Using Figure 1.1 as a guide, type the receiving address and the salutation.

    Your document will look like Figure 1.2.

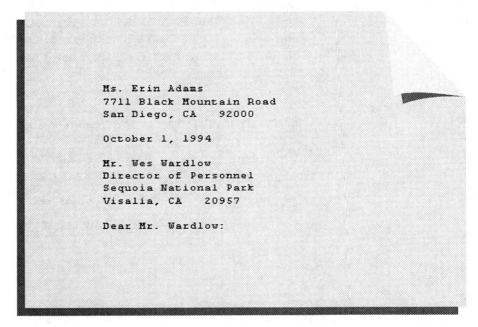

Figure 1.2

➤ **To enter paragraphs:**

1. Type the first paragraph of the document shown in Figure 1.1.

    Type the whole paragraph without stopping, even if you make a mistake. At the end of the paragraph, press [ENTER] twice.

2. In the same manner, type the second and third paragraphs, pressing [ENTER] at the appropriate places.

    As you type the second and third paragraphs, the text will be entered on lines toward the bottom of the window. When the last line on the window is filled, the word wrap feature brings a new, blank line into view at the bottom of the window as the very top line scrolls off the window. This scrolling feature allows you to create a document longer than the height of the screen or window.

3. Type the last lines of the document, including two blank lines for your signature.

> **Reminder**
> Press [ENTER] only at the end of a paragraph or to insert a blank line.

The first draft of your document is now finished. The next step is correcting the document. You need to move the insertion point to different locations in the document to correct any mistakes and make any desired revisions.

Moving Around in the Document

So far, the insertion point has been at the end of the text you've typed. The insertion point is always at a specific character position in a document. You will need to move the insertion point to the position at which you want to make a correction, insert new text, or perform some other action. You can move the insertion point by pressing the arrow keys, clicking the left mouse button, or pressing other appropriate keys. You will use the scroll bar to bring text that is off the screen back into view.

➤ **To move the insertion point using the arrow keys:**

1. Press ← on the keyboard until the insertion point is on the first character of the current line in the document.

2. Press ↑ until the insertion point is on the first line of the document.

3. Move the insertion point to any line, and then press → until the insertion point is at the end of the line.

4. Press [↓] until the insertion point is on the first line of the last paragraph.

   Move the insertion point with the arrow keys until you are comfortable using them. As you press [↑], the text scrolls down, and as you press [↓], the text scrolls up.

➤ To move the insertion point using the mouse and scroll bar:

1. Move the I-beam pointer to the first character on the last line in the document, and click the left mouse button.

   The insertion point is now repositioned.

2. Point to and drag the scroll box in the vertical scroll bar upward to bring the first part of the document into view.

   The text scrolls down, bringing the previous few lines of the document into view. The insertion point stays in the same position, moving with the text down and off the screen.

3. Move the I-beam pointer to the first character of the first line in the document, and click the left mouse button to reposition the insertion point.

4. Click the down scroll arrow on the scroll bar. Click once to move down a few lines; click and hold to scroll down several lines.

   The text scrolls up, bringing the next few lines of the document into view. The insertion point stays in the same position, moving with the text up and off the screen.

5. Click the up scroll arrow on the scroll bar.

   The text scrolls down, bringing the previous few lines of the document and insertion point into view. Move the insertion point to other locations in the document using the mouse and scroll bar until you are comfortable with these procedures.

➤ To move the insertion point using other keys:

1. Press [END] to move the insertion point to the end of the line.
2. Press [HOME] to move the insertion point to the beginning of the line.
3. Press [PGUP] to move the insertion point to the first line of text in the window.
4. Press [PGDN] to move the insertion point to the last line of text in the window.
5. Move the insertion point to any location in the document, and then press [CTRL] + [→] to move one word to the right.
6. Press [CTRL] + [←] to move one word to the left.

Other keystroke combinations are useful for moving around in the document, especially when the document is large. You can find more information on keystroke combinations by clicking the jump term *Keystrokes* in the WordPerfect Help Contents window.

Making Simple Corrections

Correcting errors in a document and adding new text is called *editing*. Many typing mistakes can be corrected by deleting characters or words and inserting new ones. Adding new text involves moving the insertion point to the desired location and typing the text. WordPerfect's preset mode of operation is *Insert mode,* in which the text is inserted automatically and pushes the existing text to the right and down. You may choose to turn Insert mode off and instead replace existing characters with new ones using *Typeover mode.* Erasing text involves moving the insertion point to the desired location and removing the text; the remaining text is pulled to the left and up to fill the space. The following steps will show you how to use these features.

➤ To type additional text:

1. Move the insertion point to the end of the last paragraph.
2. Press [SPACE] twice.
3. Type **My fax number is 999-260-0001.**

➤ To type text in Typeover mode:

1. Turn on Typeover mode by pressing [INS]

    The word *Typeover* appears at the center of the status bar, at the bottom of the screen.

2. Move the insertion point to the first character of the date on the fifth line of the document.
3. Type today's date using the same form (spelling out the month). You may also have to delete one or more characters at the end if the new date is shorter than October 1, 1994.
4. Turn off Typeover mode by pressing [INS] again.

    The word *Insert* replaces the word *Typeover* in the status bar.

➤ To delete one character:

1. Position the insertion point to the right of the last digit of the phone number.
2. Press [BKSP]

The character is erased.

3. Position the insertion point at the first digit of the phone number.

4. Press `DEL`

The character is erased.

At this point, the first and last characters of the phone number have been erased. You can erase a whole word or any amount of text by repeatedly using the `BKSP` and `DEL` keys. You will learn a quicker way to erase a word in the following steps.

> **Tip**
> Press `DEL` to erase the character at the insertion point; press `BKSP` to erase the character to the left of the insertion point.

➤ To delete a word:

1. Mouse: Move the I-beam pointer to any character in the phone number.
   or Keys: Position the insertion point on any character in the phone number.
2. Mouse: Double-click the left mouse button to select the word, and then press `DEL`
   or Keys: Press `CTRL` + `BKSP`

The entire word is erased.

You can edit your letter using the different ways to move the insertion point, to insert text, and to erase text. Try changing the text to include your own name, your major, and your phone number. As you do, you will see what editing procedures you prefer.

> **Tip**
> Move the insertion point to the desired editing location before inserting or deleting text.

SAVING THE DOCUMENT

So far, you have typed and corrected the document. The next important step is saving the document to disk using the Save command from the File menu. Saving the document to disk allows you to retrieve the document later, to alter the document further, or to print it.

You must assign a unique file name to any document you want to save. The file name may contain one to eight characters, optionally followed by a period and one to three additional characters. Do not use blank spaces. You should name the document something that reminds you of its content. Examples of file names are DANCE.LTR for a letter to a dance studio and PAPER1.MGT for your first paper in a management class. Developing clear naming conventions will be especially useful later on, when you have saved a number of documents.

The instructions in this module assume you are saving your documents on a floppy diskette in drive A:. Modify the location specification from drive A: to the appropriate drive and directory as necessary for your computer system.

> **Tip**
> A common difficulty many users have is saving a file and not knowing where it is stored. Remember to specify the drive, directory, and the file name when you save the file.

➤ **To save your document for the first time:**

1. Mouse: Point to File on the menu bar and click the left mouse button.
   or Keys: Press `ALT` + **F**

   The File menu is displayed.

2. Mouse: Point to Save in the File menu and click the left mouse button.
   or Keys: Type **S**

   When you save the document for the first time, the Save As dialog box appears as shown in Figure 1.3. The insertion point will automatically appear in the Filename text box, ready for you to enter a file name.

Creating a Document

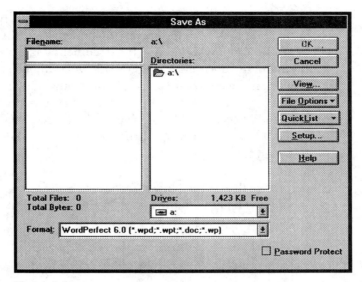

Figure 1.3

3. Type **A:\SEQUOIA.LTR** to designate drive A: as the destination disk drive and the file name as SEQUOIA.LTR, which will be stored in the root directory.

4. Select OK.

Tip
You could also save your document for the first time using the keystroke combination [CTRL] +S or the Save button on the Power Bar.

Reminder
Now that you've used the mouse to choose menu commands, select options or text, and perform actions, the numbered steps will be stated in more general terms and will look like this:
 Choose Save from the File menu
 or Select 2 as the desired line spacing

The document named SEQUOIA.LTR is now saved to disk and remains on the screen for editing. The file name appears in the title bar with the word *unmodified* after the file name. This means that the file has not been edited since the last time you saved it. At this point, you can move around in the document and edit it to your heart's content. Notice that once you have made a change in the document, you no longer see the word *unmodified* after the file name in the title bar. There are now two versions of the same document: the **current document** on the screen with the most recent editing changes and the original document saved to disk.

You can save the current document at any time, replacing the original document on disk with the current document, by using the preceding steps as your guide. You'll want to save the document you are editing every few minutes. By saving the document as you work, you will lose only the last few minutes of work if the electricity goes off, something goes wrong with your computer, or you forget to save the latest version. Because you are saving a file that has already been named, the Save As dialog box is not displayed. Once saved, the file is automatically updated when you select File Save and remains on the screen for editing.

To save the current edited document with a new name and keep the previous saved version with the former name, you will use the Save As command in the File menu. This procedure is covered in Project 2.

> **Reminder**
> Save your files frequently as you are working with them.

 If necessary, you can save your document, exit WordPerfect 6 for Windows now, and continue this project later.

Previewing the Document

When you are typing and editing a document, you can view only part of a page because the size of your document window is limited by the size of the screen. The Zoom feature of WordPerfect, located on the View menu, gives you a better idea of what the page is actually going to look like when you print it. Figure 1.4 shows your document in a Full Page zoom. The Zoom dialog box provides ways to view different parts of the document at magnification levels between 25 and 400 percent. Each time you choose a smaller percentage magnification, the text is reduced, and more of the page is visible. When you choose a larger percentage magnification, the text is enlarged, and less of the page is visible. The Zoom feature is useful, especially with longer documents in which you have made many changes and you want to make sure everything looks the way you intend before you print the document.

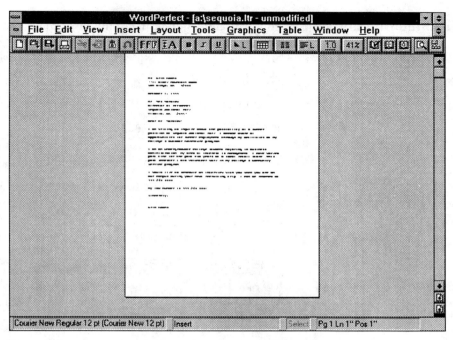

Figure 1.4

▶ To view how the printed document will appear:

1. Choose Zoom from the View menu.

   The Zoom dialog box appears as shown in Figure 1.5.

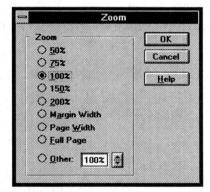

Figure 1.5

2. Select the Full Page radio button, and then select OK.

   The entire page is displayed, but the text is probably too small to read.

3. Choose Zoom from the View menu, select 75%, and then select OK.

4. Choose Zoom from the View menu, select 200%, and then select OK.

5. Use the scroll bar to bring other sections of the page into view.

You can also use the Zoom button on the Power Bar to select magnification levels.

PRINTING THE DOCUMENT

You print a document using the Print dialog box. You can choose to print the whole document or sections of the document, specify the number of copies you want, select the printer you want to use, and adjust the printing quality of text and graphics.

➤ To print the current document:

1. Check that your printer is turned on and that there is paper in it.

   If you don't know how, ask your instructor or lab assistant.

2. Choose Print from the File menu.

   The Print dialog box appears as shown in Figure 1.6.

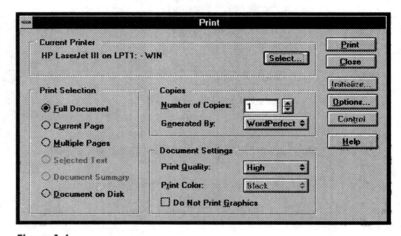

Figure 1.6

3. Select Full Document in the Print Selection list.
4. Select 1 as the desired Number of Copies.
5. Select Print.

   The document prints, and the Print dialog box automatically closes. The file remains on-screen.

Tip
You can also use the Print button on the Power Bar to display the Print dialog box.

Exiting the Current Document

When you want to stop working with the document, you need to close the document. When you choose Close from the File menu, you exit the document but remain in WordPerfect to work on other documents if you wish. You have a choice in how to exit the document. If you have edited the document since the last time you saved it, you need to decide whether or not to save it to disk, replacing the older version of the document with the newer edited version. You may want to save the edited document under a different name or in a different location; these procedures will be discussed in Project 2.

➤ **To save the edited document currently on the screen and exit that document:**

1. Choose Close from the File menu.

   If you have made any changes to the document since the last save operation, the dialog box shown in Figure 1.7 is displayed, showing the current default path and file name of the document. The dialog box is not displayed if you have not made any changes to the document since the last save operation.

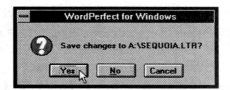

Figure 1.7

2. If this dialog box appears, select Yes.

   The document is saved to the disk, replacing the older version of the document. The screen is now clear. You can begin typing another document or exit WordPerfect.

The Next Step

This project introduced you to a three-step method for producing your word processing documents. The first step is analyzing the purpose of the document you want to write. The second step is organizing the design of the document. The third step is implementation: typing, editing, saving, and printing the document. The purpose of the document in this project was to apply for a job. The design of the letter was organized to communicate the desired information. The implementation of the letter involved the actual use of WordPerfect.

The document in this project was short. You should think about other situations in which you might need to write short documents. If you are a member of a student group, you may need to send memorandums. If you are enrolled in a literature class, you may want to type a short essay or poem. Other documents you may need to type could be much longer than the letter you typed in this project. Some examples are term papers, research reports, and the minutes of a student group meeting. In all these situations, you need to think about the purpose of the document and how it can be best organized before you start typing. After typing the document, you will want to correct any mistakes and change or rearrange the text to better communicate your ideas. Project 2 shows you more WordPerfect editing techniques that are especially useful when you are working with longer documents.

Good job. This concludes Project 1. You can either exit WordPerfect 6 for Windows or go on to work the Study Questions and Review Exercises. If you are working in a computer lab, don't forget to take your disk with you.

Summary

- Always keep in mind the purpose and the intended reader of the document you are writing.

- Design the document by deciding how to arrange the content of the document in a way that best communicates your message and can be easily understood by the reader.

- As you type the document, text automatically wraps from the end of one line to the beginning of the next line. You only press [ENTER] at the end of a paragraph or to insert a blank line.

- As more lines of text are typed, the lines at the top of the screen will scroll up and out of view. Scrolling allows you to type very long documents and then move around in the document to view any section of it on the screen.

- The insertion point is always at a specific location in the document. You can reposition the insertion point to a desired location using various combinations of the mouse, scroll bar, and keyboard keys.

- Insert mode is used to type text and move any existing text to the right and down. Typeover mode is used to replace existing text with the text being typed. The default is Insert mode.

- Press [BKSP] to erase the character preceding or to the left of the insertion point. Press [DEL] to erase the character at the insertion point.

- When you save a document, you must name the file and choose the drive and directory where you want to store it. WordPerfect uses the same file-naming rules as DOS. Remember to save your files frequently.

- You can preview the document at any time to see what it will actually look like when you print it.

- You can print a document when you want to proofread it and when you are ready to send it to the intended reader.

Key Terms and Operations

Key Terms	Operations
current document	Close
editing	Print
Insert mode	Save
paragraph	Save As
Typeover mode	Zoom

Study Questions   *MULTIPLE CHOICE*

1. Which menu contains commands that open and close a document?
   a. Help
   b. File
   c. Scroll
   d. Windows
   e. Edit

2. You can move the insertion point in the document with:
   a. the mouse.
   b. the arrow keys.
   c. [END].
   d. [HOME].
   e. All of the above.

3. To erase the character at the insertion point, press:
   a. [ENTER].
   b. [INS].
   c. [DEL].
   d. [←].
   e. [BKSP].

4. To erase a word, you could position the insertion point at any character in the word and press:
   a. [DEL].
   b. [→].
   c. [ENTER].
   d. [CTRL] + [BKSP].
   e. Help.

5. You can correct mistakes in a document:
   a. only immediately after you type the mistake.
   b. only after you have saved the document.
   c. when the document is displayed on the screen.
   d. when the document is stored to disk.
   e. with the insertion point.

6. The I-beam pointer:
   a. is the same as the insertion point.
   b. is used to choose commands from the File menu.
   c. is used to reposition the insertion point.
   d. erases text.
   e. prints text.

7. To replace text you have already typed with new text, you can:
   a. type the new text using Insert mode.
   b. type the new text using Typeover mode.
   c. press [DEL].
   d. press [CTRL] + [BKSP].
   e. press [HOME] or [END].

8. The most useful file name for the second report you might write in your history class is:
   a. ABC.WPW
   b. .002
   c. HISTORYCLASS
   d. HISTORY.002
   e. CLASS002.HISTORY

9. When you use the Save command in the File menu to save the current document to disk:
   a. the current document is erased from the screen.
   b. the current document replaces the original document on disk.
   c. you exit the current document.
   d. the current document is also printed.
   e. you are not able to open the document later on.

10. To print a document:
    a. you must first preview the document on the screen.
    b. you use the Print command in the File menu.
    c. the insertion point must be at the beginning of the document.
    d. you must print the entire document.
    e. you must have corrected all the mistakes in the document.

SHORT ANSWER

1. Describe the components of a letter.
2. Name the procedures involved in creating a document.
3. In this project you created a letter. What other types of documents can be created in WordPerfect?
4. Why is it a good idea to preview a document before printing it?
5. Why is it important to save a document?

REVIEW EXERCISES

Review the concepts presented in Project 1 by completing the following.

Developing a Short Newspaper Article

You have been asked to write a short newspaper article for the local newspaper. The article describes the need for restoration of the area around the General Sherman Tree.

1. Open a blank document window, and enter the text shown in Figure 1.8.

CREATING A DOCUMENT

```
For the Love of Giants
Won't you help? Even a giant needs tender, loving care --
especially the largest of the giants. The General Shermun Tree in
Sequoia National Park is not only bigger than any other giant
seqouia, it is, in fact, the largest living thing on earth!
Its size, however, has not protected it from overly enthusiastic
admirers.
Visitors have marveled at its bulk for over 100 years. THey
parked their wagons -- and later, autos -- on its roots; took
pieces of its bark for souvenirs, and over time, by repeatedly
touching it, literally wore away its spongy bark.
The General Shermun Tree itself is now protected by an attractive
fence, but the surrounding area has not fared as well. Two many
human feet have compacted the earth around nearby sequaias;
trails have eroded and developed holes; exhibits are incomplete.
Maintenance funds are simply inadequate to do the job. The
neighborhood of the largest living being needs touching up!
NPS protection began in 1890. Fences were built; soil worn away
from its roots was replaced. And over time, the tree's fortunes
improved.
But problems remain. Travelers from world-wide, more than
1,000,000 of them annually, visit the tree. The park needs
$150,000 to repair and relocate trails, build fences, and
construct exhibits and parking areas that will make the tree
accessible while protecting it for future generations.
```

Figure 1.8

Type the article as shown, including the mistakes. You will learn how to correct them in Project 2.

2. Save the article to your disk under the name SHERMAN.DOC. You will use this document in Project 2.

3. Edit the article, correcting any mistakes, but do not save the corrected document.

4. Close the document.

COMPETENCY TESTING

- Review the Topic Objectives to ensure you have mastered all skills listed.
- Check off:
    - Your completed Project work (the file SEQUOIA.LTR).
    - Your completed Multiple Choice exercises.
    - Your completed Review Exercises (the file SHERMAN.DOC and your TDL).
- Examine the **Creating a Document**:
    - **Project Sample Sheet** to compare your work against the sample.
    - **Multiple Choice Correct Answer Sheet** to compare your answers against the correct ones.
    - **Review Exercises Sample Answer Sheet** to compare your work against it.

Editing the Document

Topic Objectives

After completing this topic, you should be able to:

- Retrieve a document file from disk.
- Save a document under a different name.
- Find text in a document.
- Replace occurrences of specific text.
- Use the WordPerfect Speller.
- Use the WordPerfect Thesaurus.
- Copy, delete, and move selected blocks of text within a document.

Computer Tutorial

- Work through:

2.3	Opening and Saving Files (review retrieving a document file from disk and saving a document under a different name, if necessary; done last topic)
3.2	Selecting and Editing Text (review copying, deleting, and moving selected blocks of text within a document, if necessary; done last topic)
3.4.3	Find and Replace
4.2	Speller
4.4	Thesaurus

PRACTICE EXERCISES

- Read and complete all **Project 2 work** outlined on pages 42 to 59:
    - Take special note of the **Summary** and **Key Terms and Operations** sections.
    - Make sure to save the file **SHERMAN2.DOC** as indicated on **pages 46 and 58**. Be careful to use the "Save As" operation when you save this file so that you don't overwrite the original file created in the review exercises of the last topic.
- Do **Multiple Choice** exercises on pages 59 and 60.
- Do all **Review Exercises** on page 61, making sure to save the file **SERVICE.DOC**.
- Do the required **Topic Directory Listing** (TDL).

PROJECT 2: EDITING THE DOCUMENT

CASE STUDY: WRITING A NEWSPAPER ARTICLE

You learned simple editing techniques in Project 1. The more powerful editing techniques you will learn in this project are especially useful when you are typing longer, more complex documents.

After you type the initial draft of any document, as you did in Project 1, you need to reread the document and decide whether or not the document communicates the intended meaning to the reader. *Readability* and *emphasis* are two features of your message that you can usually improve. **Readability** refers to how well a reader understands your message. **Emphasis** refers to attracting the reader's attention to particular important ideas in the document.

For this second project, imagine that you have been asked to write a short newspaper article to inform the general public about the need to rehabilitate the General Sherman Tree area in Sequoia National Park. You typed the draft of this document in an assignment in Project 1. Now you want to edit the document to improve its readability.

DESIGNING THE SOLUTION

You can enhance the readability of your document in many ways. You should make sure the information in your document is correct. All the words should be spelled correctly. You could consider using a different choice of words to explain an idea and rewriting sentences and paragraphs to be more concise. You could try modifying the sequence of ideas in the document so that the intended message is clearer to the reader. In general, you want to improve the overall grammatical structure of the document. Figure 2.1 shows the Sherman document with the editing improvements you will be working on in this project.

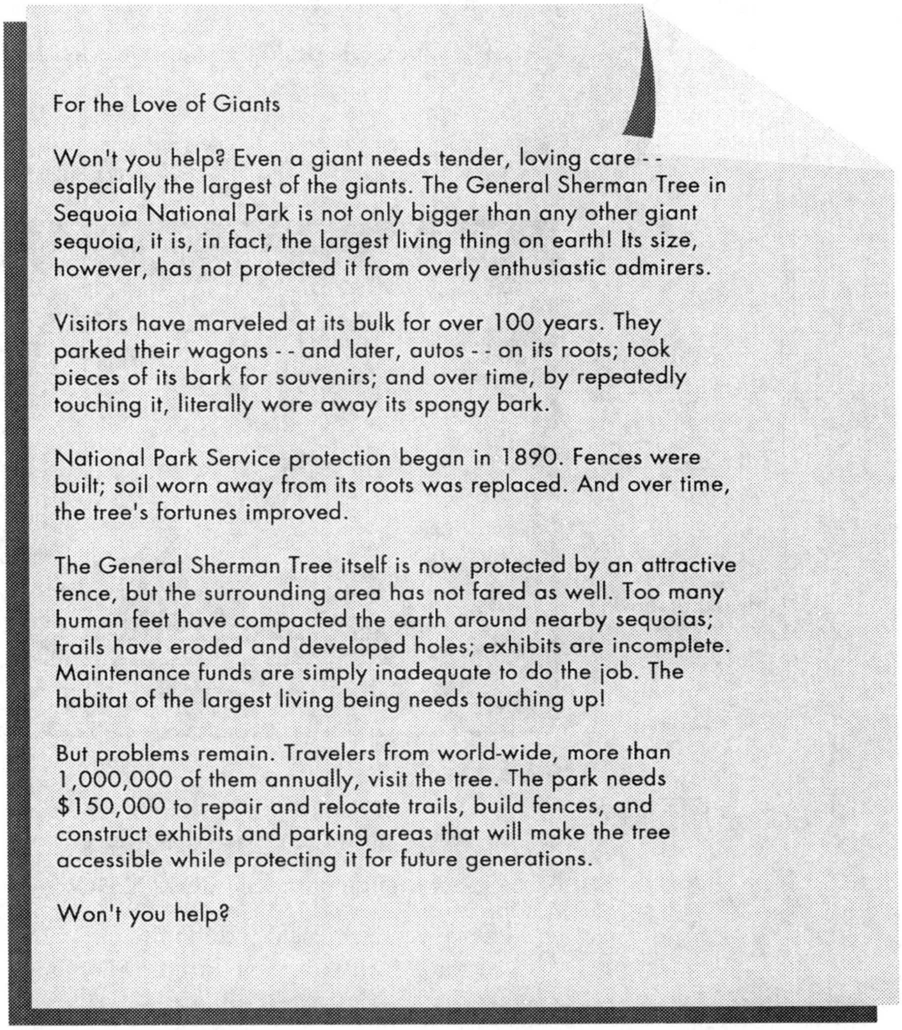

For the Love of Giants

Won't you help? Even a giant needs tender, loving care - - especially the largest of the giants. The General Sherman Tree in Sequoia National Park is not only bigger than any other giant sequoia, it is, in fact, the largest living thing on earth! Its size, however, has not protected it from overly enthusiastic admirers.

Visitors have marveled at its bulk for over 100 years. They parked their wagons - - and later, autos - - on its roots; took pieces of its bark for souvenirs; and over time, by repeatedly touching it, literally wore away its spongy bark.

National Park Service protection began in 1890. Fences were built; soil worn away from its roots was replaced. And over time, the tree's fortunes improved.

The General Sherman Tree itself is now protected by an attractive fence, but the surrounding area has not fared as well. Too many human feet have compacted the earth around nearby sequoias; trails have eroded and developed holes; exhibits are incomplete. Maintenance funds are simply inadequate to do the job. The habitat of the largest living being needs touching up!

But problems remain. Travelers from world-wide, more than 1,000,000 of them annually, visit the tree. The park needs $150,000 to repair and relocate trails, build fences, and construct exhibits and parking areas that will make the tree accessible while protecting it for future generations.

Won't you help?

Figure 2.1

OPENING A DOCUMENT

You can only edit a document that is currently on the screen. To edit a previously saved document, you must open it in a document window. When you choose Open from the File menu, WordPerfect displays a copy of the desired document in a new document window. The original document remains stored on disk. You can have as many as nine documents open in different windows at one time.

➤ To open the document SHERMAN.DOC:

1. Place your disk in drive A:.

2. Choose Open from the File menu.

   The Open File dialog box appears as shown in Figure 2.2.

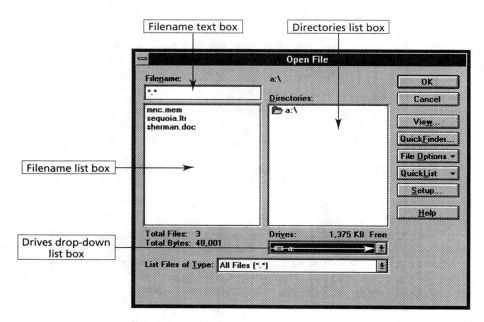

Figure 2.2

3. Select a: from the Drives drop-down list box.
4. Select the file name SHERMAN.DOC.

   Once you have selected the file name from the Filename list box, it is automatically displayed in the Filename text box.

5. Select the View button.

   A window displays the contents of the selected file, as shown in Figure 2.3. This is a handy way of making sure you are really choosing the file you intend to edit.

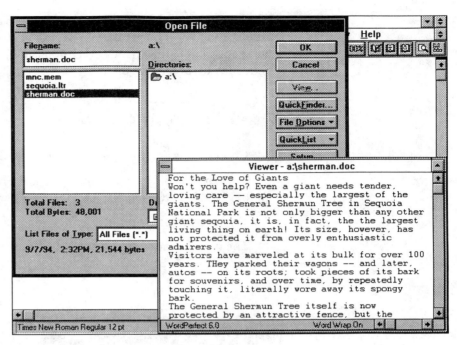

Figure 2.3

6. Choose Close from the Control-menu box in the upper-left corner of the Viewer window.

   The Viewer window disappears.

7. Select OK in the Open File dialog box.

   An hourglass icon is displayed while the file is being copied from disk. After a few seconds, when the file is loaded, the Open File dialog box disappears, and the document SHERMAN.DOC is opened.

Saving the Document Under a Different Name

You will do a lot of editing in this project. Whenever you make any kind of editing change to a document you previously had saved to disk, you should realize that you are only making those changes to the document displayed on the screen, the current document, and not simultaneously to the document on the disk. As discussed in Project 1, when you save the current document to the disk, the old version of the document is replaced by the current edited version.

In certain situations, you may want to save the current document but also keep the original version on disk unchanged; this requires you to give the current document a different name. In other situations, you might want to save the current document to a different disk or subdirectory than the original version; this requires you to type the new location specification. In both cases, you use the Save As command from the File menu.

The following Save As procedure saves the current document

SHERMAN.DOC that you will edit in this project under the name SHERMAN2.DOC. If later on you decide you don't like the editing changes you've made in SHERMAN2.DOC, you can open SHERMAN.DOC, the original document, and begin again.

➤ To save SHERMAN.DOC as SHERMAN2.DOC:

1. Choose Save As from the File menu.

   The Save As dialog box appears. The current document file name, SHERMAN.DOC, is displayed in the Filename text box.

2. Type **SHERMAN2.DOC**

   The old file name is replaced by the new file name as you type, as shown in Figure 2.4.

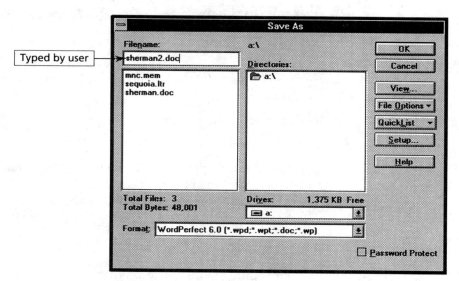

Figure 2.4

If you want to save the file in another location, select the desired disk from the Drives list box and the desired directory from the Directories list box. This information is then placed in the Filename text box automatically.

3. Select OK when you are ready.

FINDING AND REPLACING TEXT

Whenever you need to edit text in a document, you must move the insertion point to the text to be edited. In Project 1, you learned a few techniques for moving the insertion point. You can also move the insertion point by having WordPerfect find the desired location and automatically replace the text if you desire. Having WordPerfect search for and replace text is a big time-saver, especially when you are working with long documents such as term papers.

You can use the Find command from the Edit menu if you want to find the text to be edited and then do the editing manually. You can also use the Replace command from the Edit menu if you want WordPerfect to erase a portion of the text and insert new text in its place. In either case, you are asked to type the *character string* you want to locate. The character string can be a word, a phrase, or a sequence of characters within a word. The search always begins at the insertion point and proceeds either forward or backward in the document, as you wish. After the first occurrence of the character string is found, you can edit the text, search for the next occurrence of the character string, or perform any other word processing activity.

Figure 2.5 shows the SHERMAN2.DOC file containing the errors that can be corrected easily using the Find and Replace commands.

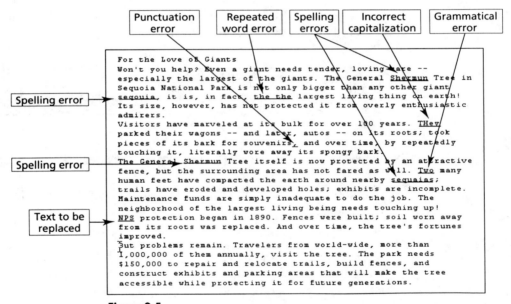

Figure 2.5

➤ To find occurrences of a particular word and edit manually:

1. Move the insertion point to the very beginning of the document.
2. Choose Find from the Edit menu.

    The Find Text dialog box appears as shown in Figure 2.6.

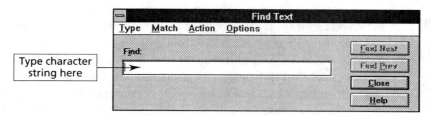

Figure 2.6

3. Type **Shermun** in the Find text box.
4. Select Find Next.

   The first appearance of the word *Shermun* is selected.

5. Select Close.

   The Find Text dialog box disappears, and the insertion point is placed immediately after the first appearance of the word *Shermun*.

6. Edit *Shermun*, replacing *u* with *a*, using the techniques you learned in Project 1.

   Repeat steps 2 through 6 as many times as necessary to correct other occurrences of the word *Shermun*. The insertion point remains at the last location and a message box displays the message "Shermun" Not Found when no additional occurrences are found.

▶ **To find several occurrences of a particular word and replace them automatically:**

1. Move the insertion point to the beginning of the SHERMAN2.DOC document.
2. Choose Replace from the Edit menu.

   The Find and Replace Text dialog box appears, as shown in Figure 2.7. You need to type the character string you want to find and replace. You also need to type the replacement text—the text you would otherwise have to type manually.

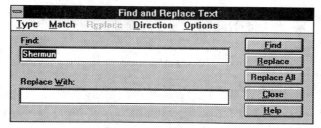

Figure 2.7

3. Type **NPS** in the Find text box (which replaces "Shermun" previously there) and press `TAB`

   The insertion point moves to the Replace With text box.

4. Type **National Park Service** in the Replace With text box.

5. Select Find.

   With this step, the search begins. The first instance of *NPS* is selected.

6. Select Replace.

   The selected text is deleted, and the new text is inserted. WordPerfect then automatically searches for the next occurrence of *NPS*. No other instances of *NPS* occur in this document, so a Find and Replace information box is displayed, as shown in Figure 2.8.

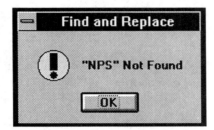

Figure 2.8

7. Select OK in the Find and Replace information box.
8. Select Close in the Find and Replace Text dialog box.

The Replace All button in the Find and Replace Text dialog box replaces every occurrence of the text automatically. This feature is also referred to as ***global search and replace.*** You can use this feature to your advantage in situations when, instead of typing the same long word or phrase over and over again, you can type a unique character string and then later do a global search and replace. However, you must be very sure of what text you want to replace so as to avoid deleting text that you didn't intend to replace. When you use global search and replace, you cannot confirm each replacement occurrence with the Replace button.

EXIT If necessary, you can save your document, exit WordPerfect 6 for Windows now, and continue this project later.

Using the WordPerfect Speller

The WordPerfect *Speller* is a *spell-checking* feature that provides a special way to search and replace misspelled text. The Speller compares each word in your document with its internal dictionary of 125,000 English-language words. If a word is not found in the dictionary, it is selected, and alternative spellings are listed. You can select one of the alternatives or manually edit the misspelled word.

A word may be highlighted as a misspelling even though it is actually correct. This occurs because the internal dictionary does not contain all words, such as proper names, acronyms, and abbreviations. The word *Sherman* is an example of a proper name not in the WordPerfect dictionary. Words in languages other than English are not in the WordPerfect dictionary, but dictionaries for other languages are available. You can also create your own personalized dictionaries; this feature is useful for storing proper names, acronyms, and specialized terms used in your courses or line of work.

The Speller also checks for repeated words and inconsistent capitalization.

For the following numbered steps, you will continue using the SHERMAN2.DOC document.

➤ **To use the Speller:**

1. Choose Speller from the Tools menu.

   The Speller dialog box appears as shown in **Figure 2.9**.

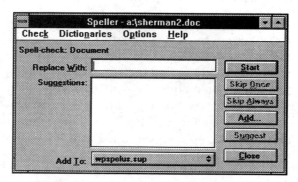

Figure 2.9

2. Choose Document from the Check menu.

   This step ensures that the whole document will be checked, regardless of the location of the insertion point.

3. Select Start.

   The first word selected as a misspelling is *Sherman*, a proper name that you previously edited. This is an example of a word that is spelled correctly but is not in the dictionary. Notice the Suggestions list box, which offers alternative spellings.

4. Select Skip Always.

Other occurrences of *Sherman* in the document will be treated as correctly spelled words, even though they are not in the dictionary. The next word selected is *seqouia*. Figure 2.10 shows the Speller dialog box with the list of alternative spellings. You can scroll through the suggestions list.

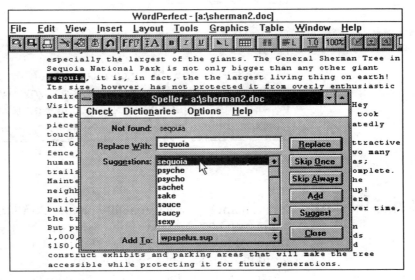

Figure 2.10

5. Select the correct spelling, *sequoia*, from the Suggestions list box.

   The word *sequoia* appears in the Replace With text box.

6. Select Replace.

   The selected text is deleted and the new text is inserted in the document. The next occurrence of a misspelling is a double occurrence of the word *the*, which is indicated in the Speller dialog box.

7. Select Replace.

   The next misspelling is *THey*, an example of incorrect capitalization, which is indicated in the Speller dialog box.

8. Select *They* in the Suggestions list box.

9. Select Replace.

10. Continue to spell-check your version of the SHERMAN2.DOC document.

    The Speller question box, shown in Figure 2.11, is displayed when the Speller finds no other misspellings in the document.

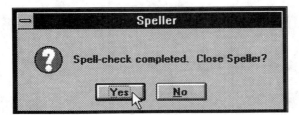

Figure 2.11

11. Select Yes.

> **Tip**
> When the correct spelling is not in the Suggestions list box, you can type a new spelling in the Replace With text box and select Suggest to see a new list of alternatives.

> **Tip**
> The Speller does not recognize the misuse of a word as a misspelling; the sentence beginning with *Two many human feet* is one example. Also, the Speller does not recognize punctuation errors, such as using a comma instead of a semicolon.

Using the Thesaurus

You can improve the readability of your document by using different words to express an idea. You may know what you are trying to say but are having trouble thinking of the best word to use. Or you might be overusing the same word in the document, which is boring to the reader. The WordPerfect Thesaurus is very useful in these situations.

The ***Thesaurus*** is a dictionary of synonyms and antonyms. You can use the Thesaurus to search for synonyms and antonyms of a word in your document and then replace the word with the desired synonym or antonym. You can also search for synonyms and antonyms of other words in the Thesaurus that are marked with bullets, called ***headwords***. The Thesaurus is an interesting tool to use, and it helps to build your vocabulary.

You will continue to edit the SHERMAN2.DOC document, looking for a synonym for the word *neighborhood* in the third paragraph.

➤ **To search for a synonym for a word:**

1. Place the insertion point on any character in the word *neighborhood*.
2. Choose Thesaurus from the Tools menu.

    The Thesaurus dialog box appears, as shown in Figure 2.12.

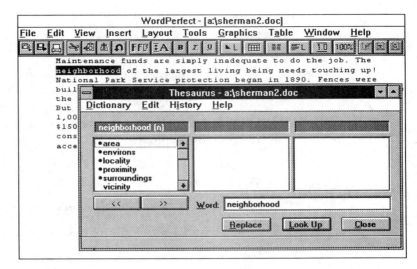

Figure 2.12

The word *neighborhood* is the headword of the left list box, which displays synonyms for that word.

(Note: If the WordPerfect you are using has a different dictionary selected than the one used to create this text, then "neighborhood" may not be found. To fix, change the spelling in your document to "neighourhood", then try again.)

3. Scroll up and down the list box to view the various choices you have.

4. Double-click *surroundings*.

   The word *surroundings* is displayed in the Word text box and as the headword in the second list box, along with a list of synonyms, as shown in Figure 2.13.

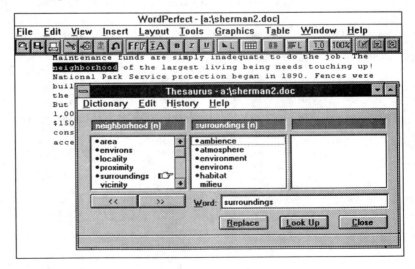

Figure 2.13

5. Select *habitat*.

6. Select Look Up.

   The two list boxes are cleared, *habitat* is now the headword of the left list box, and a list of synonyms for it is listed. You can continue to search for just the right word using the techniques in steps 4 through 6. You can also use the History menu in the Thesaurus dialog box to return to a list of previous synonyms.

7. Assuming you like the word *habitat*, select *habitat* to display it in the Word text box.

8. Select Replace to delete *neighborhood* and insert *habitat*.

9. The Thesaurus dialog box closes automatically after selecting Replace.

Practice using the Thesaurus, the Speller, and the Find and Replace commands so that you become comfortable using these editing tools.

If necessary, you can save your document, exit WordPerfect 6 for Windows now, and continue this project later.

Selecting Text

Another way of improving the readability of your document is to rearrange the sequence of ideas in the document to better emphasize the intended message to the reader. Much of the editing of a document involves changing and rearranging *blocks* of text. Think of a block as any rectangle of text. The largest block is your document and the smallest a single character. Usually, you will want to manipulate a word, phrase, sentence, or paragraph as a block. The important point is that you *select* the text to be included in a block by dragging the pointer from the beginning to the end of the text. Once the block is selected, you can delete, copy, move, or manipulate the text in other ways. In this project, you will delete, copy, and move blocks of text.

You will continue working on the SHERMAN2.DOC document.

➤ To select and deselect a block of text by dragging:

1. Move the pointer to the beginning of the first paragraph starting with *Won't you help?*

2. Press and hold down the left mouse button.

3. Drag the pointer to the end of the first sentence.

4. Release the mouse button.

   Figure 2.14 shows the selected block of text.

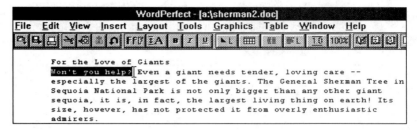

Figure 2.14

As long as you continue pressing the mouse button, text will be selected. You can also *deselect* text by dragging the pointer in the opposite direction. After you release the mouse button, you can deselect the block by pressing and releasing the mouse button.

You can quickly select a single word as a block by moving the insertion point to any character in the word and double-clicking the left mouse button. You will frequently want to select a sentence or a paragraph as a block. A quick way of doing this is to use the Select command.

▶ To select a sentence or a paragraph as a block:

1. Move the insertion point to any position in a particular sentence or paragraph.
2. Choose Select from the Edit menu.
3. Select Sentence or Paragraph from the pull-down menu.

    The sentence or paragraph is now selected as a block. You can deselect the block by pressing and releasing the mouse button.

> **Tip**
> You can also select a sentence by triple-clicking anywhere in the sentence. You can select a paragraph by quadruple-clicking anywhere in the paragraph.

Deleting Blocks of Text

In Project 1, you learned to delete text, one character or word at a time, by using `DEL`, `BKSP`, and `CTRL` + `BKSP`. If you want to delete a larger portion of text, it is easier to select the block of text and press `DEL`. The entire block is erased at one time, regardless of the size of the block. If you made a mistake or change your mind and don't want to erase the block, you can use the Undelete command to reverse the delete process. You can undelete any of the three most recent deletions.

For the following steps, you will still be using the SHERMAN2.DOC document.

▶ **To delete the first sentence in the first paragraph:**

1. Select the sentence *Won't you help?* as a block.
2. Press `DEL` or `BKSP`

   The text is now erased.

▶ **To undelete the most recent deletion:**

1. Move the insertion point to the desired location to reinsert the block.
2. Choose Undelete from the Edit menu.

   The most recently deleted block is displayed at the insertion point, and the Undelete dialog box appears as shown in Figure 2.15.

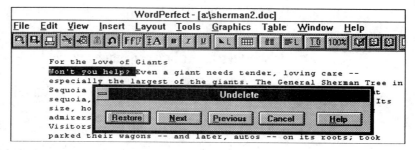

Figure 2.15

3. Select Restore to reinsert the text.

   The Previous and Next buttons in the Undelete dialog box enable you to cycle through the three most recent deletions.

> **Tip**
> Choose Undo from the Edit menu to reverse the most recent editing change. Choose Undelete to restore any of the three most recent deletions.

MOVING AND COPYING BLOCKS OF TEXT

Moving text involves deleting a block of text in one location of the document and reinserting it at another location in the same or another document. *Copying text* is duplicating a block of text at another location in the same or another document.

The procedures to move or copy a block of text within the same document are very similar. You will use the Cut and Paste commands to move selected text, and the Copy and Paste commands to duplicate selected text. When you use the Cut and Paste commands the selected block of text is moved from its original location to a new one you select. The Copy and Paste commands duplicate a highlighted block of text, save it in a temporary storage area called the *Clipboard,* and place the duplicate in a location you choose without deleting the original.

In the following steps, you will continue working with the SHERMAN2.DOC document. You will move some paragraphs to improve the sequence of ideas in the document.

➤ To move a paragraph:

1. Select the paragraph beginning with *National Park Service,* as shown in Figure 2.16.

```
For the Love of Giants
Won't you help? Even a giant needs tender, loving care --
especially the largest of the giants. The General Sherman Tree in
Sequoia National Park is not only bigger than any other giant
sequoia, it is, in fact, the largest living thing on earth! Its
size, however, has not protected it from overly enthusiastic
admirers.
Visitors have marveled at its bulk for over 100 years. They
parked their wagons -- and later, autos -- on its roots; took
pieces of its bark for souvenirs, and over time, by repeatedly
touching it, literally wore away its spongy bark.
The General Sherman Tree itself is now protected by an attractive
fence, but the surrounding area has not fared as well. Two many
human feet have compacted the earth around nearby sequoias;
trails have eroded and developed holes; exhibits are incomplete.
Maintenance funds are simply inadequate to do the job. The
habitat of the largest living being needs touching up!
National Park Service protection began in 1890. Fences were
built; soil worn away from its roots was replaced. And over time,
the tree's fortunes improved.
But problems remain. Travelers from world-wide, more than
1,000,000 of them annually, visit the tree. The park needs
$150,000 to repair and relocate trails, build fences, and
construct exhibits and parking areas that will make the tree
accessible while protecting it for future generations.
```

Figure 2.16

2. Choose Cut from the Edit menu.
3. Move the insertion point to the beginning of the third paragraph, which starts with *The General Sherman Tree.*

4. Choose Paste from the Edit menu.

➤ To copy a sentence:

1. Select the sentence *Won't you help?*
2. Choose Copy from the Edit menu.
3. Move the insertion point to the very end of the document.
4. Choose Paste from the Edit menu.

Figure 2.17 shows the results of copying and moving the blocks within the same document. If necessary, redo the spacing between words and lines after copying and moving to make the document resemble Figure 2.17.

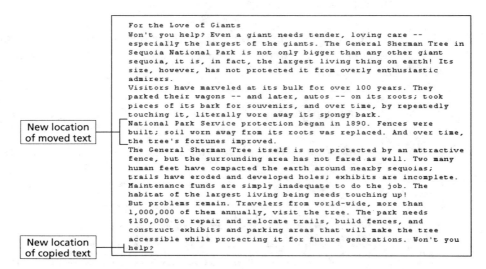

Figure 2.17

5. Choose Close from the File menu and then select Yes to save SHERMAN2.DOC.

The Next Step

You should practice the various editing techniques covered in this project. It is important to feel comfortable with these procedures and to develop insight about when to use a particular editing technique to improve your efficiency and the quality of the document. Insert a blank line between paragraphs to improve the readability of the document. Try to improve the wording in certain sentences. Experiment with different sequencing of the paragraphs. Make sure you save your document.

This concludes Project 2. You can either exit WordPerfect or go on to work the Study Questions and Review Exercises.

Summary

- You can improve the readability and emphasis of a document through WordPerfect's advanced editing features.

- If you want to edit an existing document, you must open it from a file stored on disk.

- You can use the View command in the Open File dialog box to look at the contents of your document without making changes.

- The Find and Replace commands help you move through a document efficiently to make editing changes.

Editing the Document

- You can use the Speller to check any or all words in the document and to edit any misspellings not in the Speller's dictionary.

- The Thesaurus lets you look up alternative words you might use to express an idea.

- You can select blocks of text on which to perform some action. You can delete and undelete, copy, or move blocks of text within the same document or between documents.

- You can save an edited document with a different file name than that of the original file.

Key Terms and Operations

Key Terms

block	Speller
character string	Thesaurus
Clipboard	
copying text	**Operations**
deselect	Copy
emphasis	Cut
global search and replace	Find
headword	Open
moving text	Paste
readability	Replace
select	Select
spell-checking	Undelete

Study Questions

MULTIPLE CHOICE

1. A block of text can be:
   - a. a character.
   - b. a word.
   - c. a sentence.
   - d. a paragraph.
   - e. All of the above.

2. To edit a document stored on disk, you must:
   - a. open the document.
   - b. use the Speller.
   - c. print the document first.
   - d. locate a particular character string.
   - e. copy blocks of text.

3. What command do you use to search for text in a document without looking through the document yourself?
   - a. Undo
   - b. Delete
   - c. Edit
   - d. Find
   - e. Replace

4. What command do you use to search for text in a document, delete the text, and insert new text?
   - a. Undo
   - b. Delete
   - c. Edit
   - d. Find
   - e. Replace

5. *The The* is an example of a double occurrence of the same word. To correct this type of mistake in a document, you use the:
   a. File menu.
   b. Edit menu.
   c. Move command.
   d. Speller.
   e. Thesaurus.

6. You can search for a different word to use in place of an already typed word in a document by using WordPerfect's:
   a. File menu.
   b. Edit menu.
   c. Search command.
   d. Speller.
   e. Thesaurus.

7. The quickest way to delete a paragraph is to:
   a. use `DEL` as many times as necessary to erase each character.
   b. use `CTRL` + `BKSP` as many times as necessary to erase each word.
   c. select the paragraph and press `DEL`.
   d. use the Find command.
   e. use the Undo command.

8. Which two commands do you use to make the second paragraph of a document become the fifth paragraph?
   a. Cut and Edit
   b. Cut and Paste
   c. Copy and Paste
   d. Copy and Save
   e. Cut and Save

9. What command do you use to save the current document to disk without replacing the original version of the document?
   a. Save
   b. Clipboard
   c. Replace
   d. Save As
   e. Open

10. Replicating a block of text at another location in a document is called:
    a. moving.
    b. global search and replace.
    c. readability.
    d. copying.
    e. replacing.

SHORT ANSWER

1. What is the difference between copying and moving text?
2. What happens to a block of text if it is deleted or cut?
3. What is the difference between Undelete and Undo?
4. When would you use the Find feature?
5. What dangers do you need to be aware of when using the Replace command?
6. What three types of spelling errors does WordPerfect's Speller recognize?
7. Where can you find more information about the Speller and Thesaurus in the Help feature?

Review Exercises

Review the concepts presented in Project 2 by completing the following.

Developing an Announcement

Your college has many volunteer projects available for students so they can do work in the community and receive class credit. Type the announcement shown in Figure 2.18. This announcement will be posted by your college's Community Service Office.

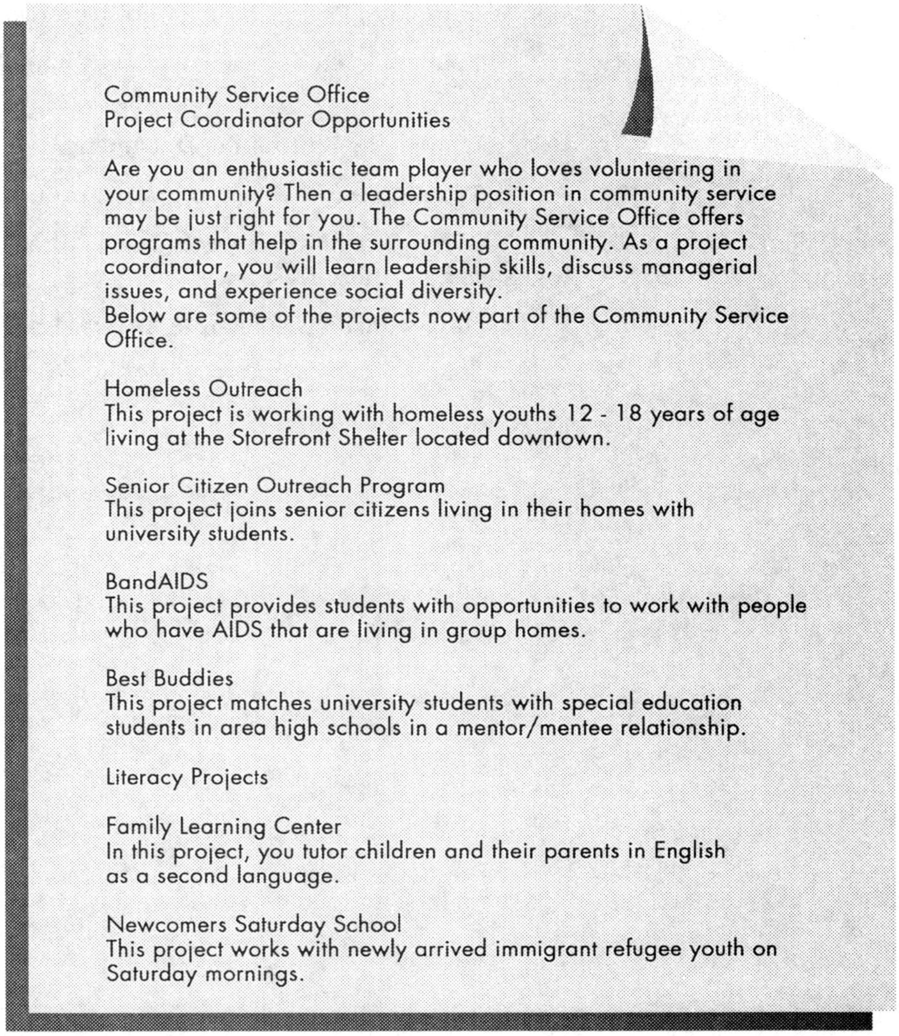

> Community Service Office
> Project Coordinator Opportunities
>
> Are you an enthusiastic team player who loves volunteering in your community? Then a leadership position in community service may be just right for you. The Community Service Office offers programs that help in the surrounding community. As a project coordinator, you will learn leadership skills, discuss managerial issues, and experience social diversity.
> Below are some of the projects now part of the Community Service Office.
>
> Homeless Outreach
> This project is working with homeless youths 12 - 18 years of age living at the Storefront Shelter located downtown.
>
> Senior Citizen Outreach Program
> This project joins senior citizens living in their homes with university students.
>
> BandAIDS
> This project provides students with opportunities to work with people who have AIDS that are living in group homes.
>
> Best Buddies
> This project matches university students with special education students in area high schools in a mentor/mentee relationship.
>
> Literacy Projects
>
> Family Learning Center
> In this project, you tutor children and their parents in English as a second language.
>
> Newcomers Saturday School
> This project works with newly arrived immigrant refugee youth on Saturday mornings.

Figure 2.18

1. Open a new document window.
2. Type the document.
3. Use the Speller to check for misspelled words.
4. Move paragraphs to improve readability.
5. Save the document as SERVICE.DOC. You will use this document in Project 3.
6. Close the document.

COMPETENCY TESTING

- Review the Topic Objectives to ensure you have mastered all skills listed.
- Check off:
    - Your completed Project work (the file SHERMAN2.DOC).
    - Your completed Multiple Choice exercises.
    - Your completed Review Exercises (the file SERVICE.DOC and your TDL).
- Examine the **Editing the Document**:
    - **Project Sample Sheet** to compare your work against the sample.
    - **Multiple Choice Correct Answer Sheet** to compare your answers against the correct ones.
    - **Review Exercises Sample Answer Sheet** to compare your work against it.

Formatting the Document

Topic Objectives

After completing this topic, you should be able to:

- Reveal formatting codes.
- Set margins.
- Justify text.
- Set tabs (*Note:* Covered in Practice Exercises *only*).
- Indent paragraphs (*Note:* Covered in Practice Exercises *only*).
- Set line spacing.
- Insert page breaks (*Note:* Covered in Practice Exercises *only*).

Computer Tutorial

- Work through:
  - 3.3   Codes
  - 3.4.2 Justification and Spacing
  - 3.5.1 The Ruler Bar

Practice Exercises

- Read and complete all **Project 3 work** outlined on pages 64 to 87:
  - Take special note of the **Summary** and **Key Terms and Operations** sections.
  - Make sure to save the file **SERVICE2.DOC** as indicated on page 86. Be careful to use the "Save As" operation when you save this file so that you don't overwrite the original file created in the review exercises of the last topic.
- Do **Multiple Choice** exercises on pages 87 and 88.
- Do all **Review Exercises** on pages 89 and 90, making sure to save the file **MEETING.DOC**.
- Do the required **Topic Directory Listing (TDL)**.

PROJECT 3: FORMATTING THE DOCUMENT

CASE STUDY: FORMATTING AN ANNOUNCEMENT

In Project 2, you learned how to improve the readability of a document by using a variety of editing tools. *Formatting* the document is another way of attracting the reader's attention to particular important ideas in the document and thus improving readability.

Formatting a document refers to how you lay out or arrange the text for the printed page. You can use a variety of formatting techniques to lay out text on a line, paragraph, or page, including centering and indenting text, and setting margins and line spacing. The guiding principle for formatting is to arrange the text attractively, leaving plenty of *white space,* or unprinted areas, around text to provide a visual contrast so the document does not look crowded. This design guideline is true for letters, memoranda, reports, and most other written communication.

For this third project, imagine you have been asked to design an announcement of volunteer project opportunities sponsored by your college's Community Service Office. The announcement will be posted on bulletin boards and also distributed through campus mail. You typed the draft of this document in the Review Exercises in Project 2 and saved it as SERVICE.DOC. You will improve the layout of the document in this project.

DESIGNING THE SOLUTION

You can apply formatting techniques at every major section of your document. For example, you can center the headline or title on the line, which creates white space that gives the title greater emphasis. A minimum of 1 inch for the top, bottom, left, and right margins is a standard guideline to create white space separating the text from the edges of the page. Indenting creates white space on the left and right sides of paragraphs. You can also vary the white space between lines of text. You can use the WordPerfect Ruler Bar or dialog boxes to control these formatting features.

Subheadings are titles for specific portions of the document and can be used to divide the text into visual units to help the reader focus on a particular section of the document.

Figure 3.1 shows the SERVICE.DOC document with the formatting improvements you will be working on in this project.

Community Service Office
Project Coordinator Opportunities

Are you an enthusiastic team player who loves volunteering in your community? Then a leadership position in community service may be just right for you. The Community Service Office offers programs that help in the surrounding community. Each program is coordinated by two college students. Together they organize and recruit volunteers for all the activities of the program. As a project coordinator, you will learn leadership skills, discuss managerial issues, and experience social diversity.

Below are some of the projects now part of the Community Service Office. You are encouraged to become involved and also to offer your ideas on any new issues you feel need to be addressed.

Homeless Outreach
This project is working with homeless youths 12-18 years of age living at the Storefront Shelter located downtown.

Senior Citizen Outreach Program
This project joins senior citizens living in their homes with university students.

BandAIDS
This project provides student opportunities to work with people who have AIDS and are living in group homes.

Best Buddies
This project matches university students with special education students in area high schools in a mentor/mentee relationship.

Literacy Projects

Family Learning Center
In this project, you tutor children and their parents in English as a second language.

Newcomers Saturday School
This project works with newly arrived immigrant refugee youth on Saturday mornings.

Figure 3.1

1. Open the SERVICE.DOC file. Good luck, and have fun.

Revealing Formatting Codes

It is important to realize that when you format a line, paragraph, or page, you are inserting *formatting codes* in the text at the locations where you want the formatting to take place. **Formatting codes** are instructions or commands that perform a particular function, such as indenting or ending a paragraph, beginning at the location at which they are inserted. If you change your mind and want to remove a particular type of formatting, you must delete the formatting code. The formatting codes are not displayed on the screen unless you need to see them to delete them or make sure the insertion point is positioned correctly.

When you select Reveal Codes from the View menu, the document window is divided into two areas by a horizontal double line, called the **Reveal Codes divider line.** The current document is displayed in the text area at the top of the document window. The same text is displayed in the Reveal Codes area, with the formatting codes appearing in rectangles.

> **Tip**
> Two common formatting codes are:
> [HRt] Hard return code represents movement of text to the next line after pressing ENTER. This is the code that you insert when you want to end a paragraph or insert a blank line.
> [SRt] Soft return code represents movement of text to the next line without pressing ENTER. This code is inserted by WordPerfect for word wrap.

You delete an unwanted code just as you delete any other single character in the document using DEL or BKSP.

When you move the insertion point in the current document, a rectangular insertion point, or block cursor, in the Reveal Codes area also moves and highlights the character at the corresponding location. You can change the size of the Reveal Codes area of the document window by dragging the Reveal Codes divider line.

➤ **To reveal the codes in the SERVICE.DOC document currently on the screen:**

1. Move the insertion point to the top of the document.
2. Choose Reveal Codes from the View menu.

    Check that your screen resembles Figure 3.2.

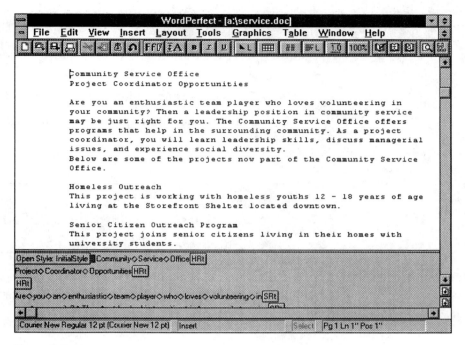

Figure 3.2

3. Move around in the document using the arrow keys or scroll bars and observe the formatting codes.

➤ To delete the third [HRt] code:

1. Move the insertion point to the first blank line.

   Observe the corresponding movement of the block cursor in the Reveal Codes area of the document window. The block cursor should be just to the left of the [HRt] code.

2. Press [DEL]

   The [HRt] code is deleted and, correspondingly, no blank line is displayed in the document.

➤ To reinsert the blank line:

1. Move the insertion point to the first character of the line beginning with *Are you*.

   You can accurately determine the location of the insertion point by observing the block cursor in the Reveal Codes area of the document window.

2. Press [ENTER]

   The [HRt] code is inserted and, correspondingly, a blank line is displayed in the document.

➤ **To change the size of the Reveal Codes area of the document window:**

1. Move the I-beam pointer to the Reveal Codes divider line—the horizontal double line between the document and the Reveal Codes area.

   The pointer changes from an I-beam to a double-arrow symbol.

2. Drag the line either up or down to increase or decrease the size of the Reveal Codes area.

> **Reminder**
> To drag means to press the left mouse button, move the pointer, and then release the button.

➤ **To close the Reveal Codes area and return to document display:**

1. Choose the View menu.

   A check mark is displayed next to the Reveal Codes menu choice to indicate that it is currently toggled on.

2. Choose Reveal Codes from the View menu.

   The check mark is erased, indicating that Reveal Codes is turned off. The Reveal Codes area disappears, and the document returns to occupy the entire window.

> **Tip**
> You can also press ALT + F3 to toggle Reveal Codes on or off.

USING THE RULER BAR

The Ruler Bar is a feature that appears as a graphic display across the top part of the document. The Ruler Bar provides an easy way to insert and move margin and tab formatting codes in your document. You can also insert margin and tab formatting codes by setting options in the appropriate dialog box, but using the Ruler Bar when you can is a time-saver. You can toggle the Ruler Bar on or off at your convenience.

> **Tip**
> You need a mouse to use the Ruler Bar.

FORMATTING THE DOCUMENT

➤ To display the Ruler Bar:

1. Choose the View menu.
2. Choose Ruler Bar to toggle on the Ruler Bar.

   The Ruler Bar is displayed below the menu bar, and below the Power Bar if it is on. Figure 3.3 shows the features of the Ruler Bar.

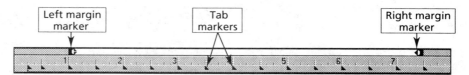

Figure 3.3

The Ruler Bar has three rows. The top row displays the *margin markers,* the arrowheads that indicate the left and right margin locations. The left margin is currently set to 1 inch and the right margin to 7.5 inches from the left edge of the paper. The second row is a ruled line in 1/8-inch increments. The 1 position on the Ruler Bar indicates 1 inch from the left edge of the paper. The third row displays the *tab markers,* the notches that indicate the current tab settings. The tabs are currently set every 1/2 inch. Changing the current margin or tab settings involves dragging the appropriate icon to the new position on the Ruler Bar.

SETTING MARGINS

Margins are the spaces between the text area and the top, bottom, and side edges of the paper. The left and right margin settings control where printing begins and ends for each line. The top and bottom margin settings control where printing begins and ends on each page. The default settings result in 1-inch margins on all sides.

You can reset the margins at any point in the document. When you reset the margins, a formatting code appears on that line. The margin setting affects all text from that line down or until you change the margins again later in the document.

Only the left and right margins can be set using the Ruler Bar. The Margins dialog box, accessed from the Layout menu, can be used to set all four margins.

➤ To set the left and right margins using the Ruler Bar:

1. Make sure the Ruler Bar is toggled on.
2. Move the insertion point to the very first position in the first line of the SERVICE.DOC document.

3. Drag the left margin marker to the 1.5-inch mark.

   Figure 3.4 shows that a dotted vertical line is displayed down the page and moves with the margin marker. This helps you visualize the desired position of the margin.

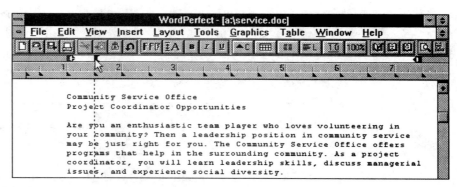

Figure 3.4

4. Drag the right margin marker to the 7-inch mark.
5. Toggle on Reveal Codes to check that [LftMar] and [RgtMar] codes are inserted at the beginning of the line.

   After looking at the results of the new margins, you may decide to change the settings again at the same line. Make sure the insertion point is in the line, and then repeat step 3 or 4. The left and right measurements in the codes are automatically modified.

To set the top and bottom margins, or if you know exactly the margin settings you want, you will use the Margins dialog box.

➤ To set margins with the Margins dialog box:

1. Move the insertion point to the first line of the SERVICE.DOC document.
2. Choose Margins from the Layout menu.

   The Margins dialog box appears, as shown in Figure 3.5. Values in the four Page Margins text boxes are in inches. The value in the Left text box is already selected.

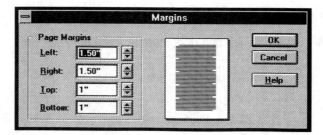

Figure 3.5

3. Type **1** to set the left margin to 1 inch.
4. Mouse: Double-click in the Right text box.
   or Keys: Press `TAB` to select the Right text box.
5. Type **1** to set the right margin to 1 inch.
6. Mouse: Double-click in the Top text box.
   or Keys: Press `TAB` to select the Top text box.
7. Type **2** to set the top margin to 2 inches.
8. Mouse: Double-click in the Bottom text box.
   or Keys: Press `TAB` to select the Bottom text box.
9. Type **.5** to set the bottom margin to one-half inch.
10. Select OK.

> **Tip**
> You can double-click anywhere in the top row of the Ruler Bar to access the Margins dialog box.

[TopMar] and [BotMar] codes are inserted at the beginning of the line (which can be seen in the Reveal Codes area). The [TopMar] and [BotMar] codes should always be placed on the first line of the page where you want the new top and bottom margin settings to take effect. Use Reveal Codes to verify the placement of the formatting codes.

Practice changing the margins with the Ruler Bar and the Margins dialog box to become comfortable using them.

EXIT If necessary, you can save your document, exit WordPerfect now, and continue this project later. Save your document as SERVICE2.DOC.

JUSTIFYING TEXT

Text *justification* refers to aligning text along the left and right margins. Four ways to justify text are illustrated in Figure 3.6, an example of a billing statement to a customer.

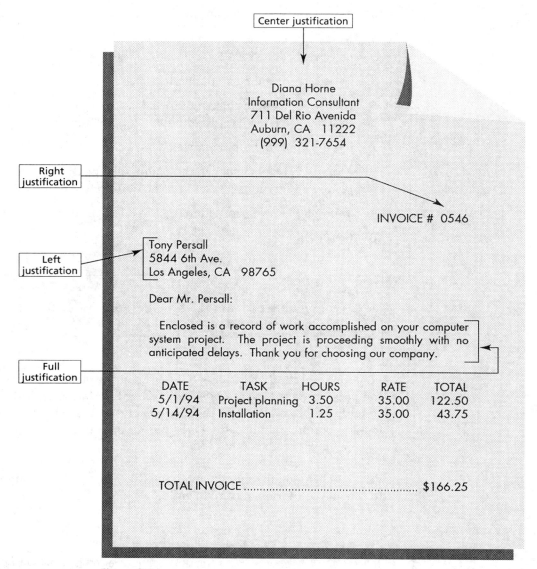

Figure 3.6

Left justification aligns text on the left margin and is commonly used for memos, initial drafts of papers, or other informal communications. Right justification aligns text on the right margin. It is especially useful for typing a right-aligned return address in a letter. Center justification aligns text around a center point between the left and right margins. You can use center justification for the title, author, and other information on the title pages of your term papers and reports. Full justification aligns text on both margins. It gives the text a rectangular appearance in contrast to the uneven or ragged right margin of left-justified text. However, full justification adds space between words to take up the slack and may present gaping holes in the lines of text. You will have to see which justification setting you prefer.

Formatting the Document

The default setting is left justification. Text justification actually affects one paragraph at a time, so when you reset text justification, you are inserting a formatting code at the beginning of a paragraph. The setting affects each paragraph from that point down, unless you change the justification setting later in the document.

To set the justification for a specific paragraph or group of paragraphs, you will select the text first and then choose the desired justification. When you justify selected text, a formatting code for the new justification is inserted at the beginning of the paragraph, changing it to the new format. Another formatting code is inserted at the end of the selected text, changing the format back to the justification previously used.

You can also center-justify a specific line of text. You will choose Line from the Layout menu and Center from the pull-down menu.

You can set text justification using the Justification button on the Power Bar or the Justification command in the Layout menu.

In the following numbered steps, you will continue editing the SERVICE.DOC document.

➤ **To center-justify the title lines of the SERVICE.DOC document using the Power Bar:**

1. Make sure the Power Bar is toggled on.
2. Select the first two title lines in the document.

3. Click and hold down the Justification button on the Power Bar.

    The Justification pull-down menu appears as shown in Figure 3.7.
4. Select Center, and then release the mouse button.

Figure 3.7

Reminder
You can click anywhere in the work area of the document window to deselect a block of text.

Using Reveal Codes, you can observe the placement of the [Just:Center] code at the beginning of the first title line of the selected text and the placement of the default [Just:Left] code at the end.

➤ To reset the title lines back to left justification using the Layout menu:

1. Place the insertion point anywhere on the first line of the title to the right of the [Just:Center] code.
2. Choose Justification from the Layout menu.

    Figure 3.8 shows the Layout Justification menu.
3. Choose Left.

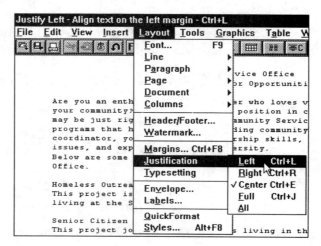

Figure 3.8

The [Just:Center] code disappears and the two title lines are now left-justified.

➤ To center-justify a line of text using the Layout menu:

1. Place the insertion point at the beginning of the line *Homeless Outreach*.
2. Choose Line from the Layout menu.
3. Choose Center from the cascading menu.

    When you center a specific line, the [Center] code is placed at the location of the insertion point. You need to be careful to place the insertion point at the beginning of the line you want to center. Repeat the steps to center-justify *Senior Citizen Outreach Program, BandAIDS, Best Buddies, Literacy Projects,* and the first two title lines.

> **Tip**
> Centering text on a line is different from centering all of the text on a page. If you would like to do the latter, simply place your insertion point at the beginning of the page, then select Page Center from the Layout menu. You can center text on the current page only or on the current page and all subsequent pages. Note that if you select the latter, you will have to remember to turn it off (using Layout Page Center) when you no longer want the feature.

Setting Tabs

Tab settings, or tabs, control the position of text from the left margin and the alignment of text at the tab location. Tab markers on the Ruler Bar indicate the location of particular tab settings. To insert a tab, you press `TAB` to move the insertion point directly to the next tab location on the current line. You set tabs by changing the position or type of tab on the Ruler Bar. Tabs are used to indent paragraphs and provide an easy way to align simple columns of text when more sophisticated tables aren't required.

Four types of tab settings are shown in Figure 3.9. A left tab behaves like left justification: text appears to the right of the tab setting. A right tab behaves like right justification: text appears to the left of the tab setting. You set a decimal-aligned tab when numbers need to be aligned on either side of a decimal point. Not shown in the figure is a center tab, which disperses text evenly on each side of the tab. Each type of tab may be preceded by a series of periods called ***dot leaders***, which can be used, for example, in a table of contents to connect titles and page numbers.

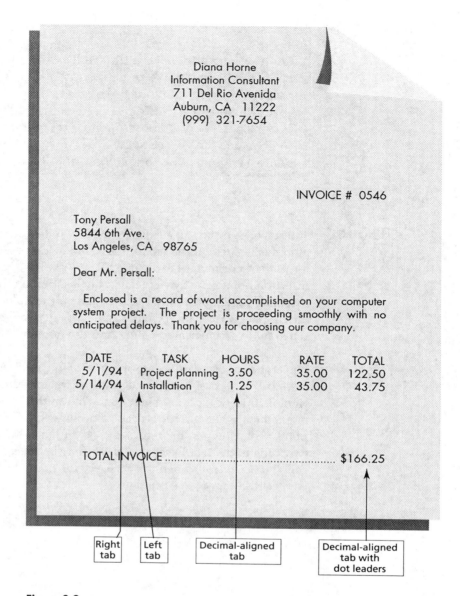

Figure 3.9

The default tab settings are left tabs located every half inch on the Ruler Bar. Tab markers can be located anywhere on the Ruler Bar. Whenever you change a tab marker, the new setting is applied at the line of the insertion point. Like other formatting codes, the Tab codes control text formatting from that point on, unless you change the tab marker later in the document. You can choose the type of tab you need by using the Tab Set button on the Power Bar. Tabs can be set directly on the Ruler Bar or by using the Tab Set command in the Line pull-down menu in the Layout menu.

In the following steps, you will continue editing the SERVICE.DOC document.

FORMATTING THE DOCUMENT

➤ **To insert a tab at each of two paragraphs in the current SERVICE.DOC document with** `TAB` **:**

1. Place the insertion point at the letter *A* in *Are you*.
2. Press `TAB`
3. Place the insertion point at the letter *B* in *Below are*.
4. Press `TAB`

   The paragraphs are properly indented at the first tab marker. Observe the location of the inserted [Left Tab] codes using Reveal Codes.

➤ **To insert a new left tab setting at the first paragraph using the Ruler Bar:**

1. Toggle on the Ruler Bar.
2. Place the insertion point at the letter *A* in *Are you*.
3. Point to the left tab marker currently set at the 1.5-inch position on the Ruler Bar.
4. Drag the left tab marker, currently set at the 1.5-inch position, to the 1.25-inch position on the Ruler Bar, as shown in Figure 3.10.

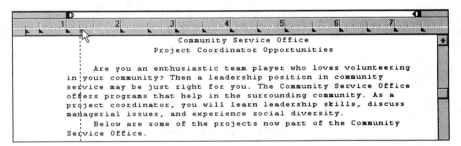

Figure 3.10

You can see in the Reveal Codes area that the [LeftTab] codes at the beginning of each of the two paragraphs now justify text to the new tab stops on the Ruler Bar.

CLEARING EXISTING TABS

You don't have to work with the default tab settings. Depending on the particular document you are typing, it may be easier to delete the existing tab settings and set new ones. You can quickly clear tab settings by dragging the tab markers off the Ruler Bar.

➤ To clear an existing tab setting from the Ruler Bar:

1. Toggle on the Ruler Bar.
2. Place the insertion point at the beginning of the line *Homeless Outreach*.
3. Move the pointer to the left tab marker at the 1.25-inch location on the Ruler Bar.
4. Drag the tab marker down off the Ruler Bar.

    That particular tab setting is deleted, and a new tab setting, a [Tab Set] code, is inserted automatically. You can verify this with Reveal Codes.

➤ To clear a group of existing tab settings from the Ruler Bar:

1. Place the insertion point at the left margin of the line *Homeless Outreach*.
2. Move the pointer to the grey area immediately to the left of the tab marker at the 2-inch location.
3. Select all the tab markers by pressing [SHFT] and the left mouse button and dragging the pointer across the Ruler Bar to highlight all the tab markers to the right of the 1-inch location and including the 7.5-inch location.
4. Release [SHFT] and the mouse button.
5. Drag the selected tab markers down off the Ruler Bar.

    The selected tab markers are deleted from the Ruler Bar, and a new tab code is inserted. You should have no tab markers to the right of the 1-inch location.

SETTING NEW TABS

You can quickly set new tabs directly on the Ruler Bar by choosing the desired type of tab on the Power Bar and then clicking at the desired location on the Ruler Bar.

➤ To set a left, a right, and a dot-leader left tab using the Power Bar and the Ruler Bar:

1. Toggle on the Power Bar.

    Observe the Tab Set button on the Power Bar. The default is a left tab.
2. Toggle on the Ruler Bar.
3. Place the insertion point at the left margin of the line *Homeless Outreach*.
4. Click on the 1.5-inch position on the Ruler Bar to set a left tab.

5. Click the Tab Set button on the Power Bar and select Right.

    A right tab is now the default of the Tab Set button on the Power Bar.

6. Click on the 3.5-inch position on the Ruler Bar to set a right tab.

7. Click the Tab Set button on the Power Bar and select ...Left.

   A dot-leader left tab is now the default of the Tab Set button.

8. Click the 5-inch position on the Ruler Bar to set a dot-leader left tab.

   A new tab code is now inserted at the beginning of the line *Homeless Outreach*. You can verify this with Reveal Codes. Your tab settings on the Ruler Bar should look like Figure 3.11.

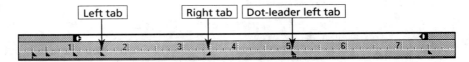

Figure 3.11

When you are typing text, you move the insertion point to the next tab marker by pressing [TAB]. When you press [TAB], you are inserting into the document the formatting code of the next tab marker in the Ruler Bar.

➤ To set new tabs in the SERVICE.DOC document using the Ruler Bar:

1. Place the insertion point at the end of the SERVICE.DOC document, after the paragraph ending with *Saturday mornings*.

2. Insert a blank line by pressing [ENTER]

3. Type **For more information call:** and press [ENTER]

4. Press [TAB] to move the cursor to the first tab marker.

5. Press [TAB] again to move the cursor to the next tab marker, which is a right tab.

6. Type **Community Service Office**

   The text moves to the left from the tab marker as you type.

7. Press [TAB] to move the cursor to the next tab marker, which is a dot-leader left tab. Notice how a series of periods are displayed "leading" to the tab.

8. Type **260-4861**

   Check that the text you just typed reflects the new tab settings, as shown in Figure 3.12.

```
Newcomers Saturday School
   This project works with newly arrived immigrant refugee youth on
Saturday mornings.

For more information call:
   Community Service Office . . . . . 260-4861
```

Figure 3.12

You can also set new tabs in the Ruler Bar using the Tab Set dialog box. In addition to clearing and setting tabs, the Tab Set dialog box enables you to type an exact position for tabs and to enter either *relative tabs*, which are measured from the left margin or *absolute tabs*, which are measured from the left edge of the paper. If you move the left margin, relative tabs will automatically move relative to the new left margin position, whereas absolute tabs will remain at the same position regardless of the left margin position.

➤ To set tabs using the Tab Set dialog box:

1. Toggle on the Ruler Bar.

   This step is not necessary to use the Tab Set dialog box but only to see the Ruler Bar being changed.

2. Move the insertion point to the end of the SERVICE.DOC document by pressing CTRL + END

3. Choose Line from the Layout menu.

4. Choose Tab Set from the cascading menu.

   Figure 3.13 shows the Tab Set dialog box. The current tabs are shown in the list box, and their measurement is relative to the left margin.

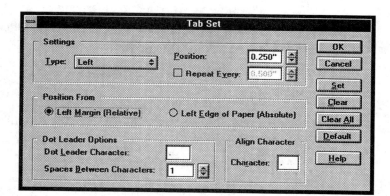

Figure 3.13

5. Select Left Edge of Paper (Absolute) in the Position From box.

   The current tabs are now absolute tabs measured from the left edge of the paper. The tab position does not change; only the beginning point of the measurement changes.

6. Select Clear All.

   All the tab markers are deleted.

7. Select Center in the Type drop-down list box.

8. Place the insertion point in the Position text box.

9. Type **4**

10. Select Set.

11. Select OK.

Observe the placement of the tab marker in the Ruler Bar. If you toggle between the two Position From options in the Tab Set dialog box, you will see that the tab marker remains in the same position on the Ruler Bar, but the measurement changes. In this case, the 4-inch absolute tab is equivalent to a 3-inch relative tab because the left margin is set at 1 inch. If you want to experiment moving the left margin around, use relative tabs because they will move relative to the left margin. If you always want the tabs to be measured from the edge of the paper no matter where the left margin is set, use absolute tabs.

INDENTING TEXT

Indenting text is justifying text on a tab rather than the left and right margins. Indentations create white space that causes the text to visually stand out against the background of the other text and attract the reader's attention. You can also use indentations to communicate the hierarchical structure of your ideas in a document, such as an outline or table of contents.

Indenting uses a tab as a temporary left margin for a paragraph. Three types of indentations are illustrated in Figure 3.14. An indent at the left margin justifies all the lines of a paragraph at a tab position. A double indent also pulls in the text on the right side of the paragraph the same distance as the left. A hanging indent indents all but the first line of the paragraph, which remains at the left margin.

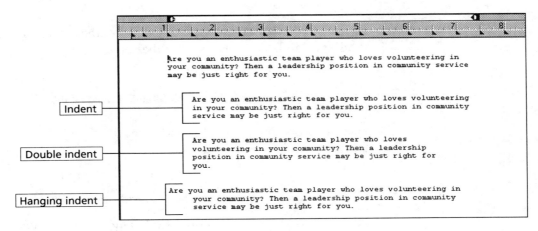

Figure 3.14

You have already learned how to indent only the first line of a paragraph by pressing TAB at the beginning of the paragraph. Since indent codes are inserted at the location of the insertion point, you must place the desired indent formatting code at the beginning of the paragraph. You will insert the desired indent code using the Paragraph command in the Layout menu.

➤ **To double-indent a paragraph one tab marker from the left margin in the SERVICE.DOC document currently on the screen:**

1. Place the insertion point at the beginning of the paragraph that starts *This project,* following *Homeless Outreach.*

2. Choose Paragraph from the Layout menu.

    Figure 3.15 shows the Paragraph cascading menu.

3. Choose Double Indent.

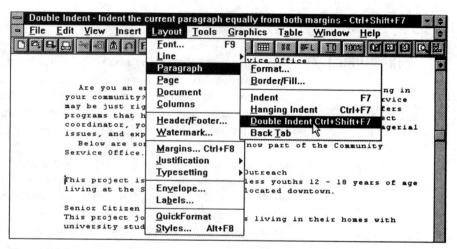

Figure 3.15

4. Repeat steps 1–3 to double-indent the text of the Senior Citizen Outreach Program, BandAIDS, and Best Buddies paragraphs.

➤ **To give a paragraph in the SERVICE.DOC document a hanging indent:**

1. Place the insertion point at the end of the line *Family Learning Center.* This line is an example of a subheading.

2. Delete the [HRt] code to form one longer paragraph.

3. Press SPACE twice to separate the subheading from the text.

4. Place the insertion point on the *F* (in *Family*) at the beginning of the paragraph.

5. Choose Paragraph from the Layout menu.

6. Choose Hanging Indent from the cascading menu.

    The reformatted paragraph is shown in Figure 3.16.

```
                    Literacy Projects
Family Learning Center - In this project, you tutor children and
         their parents in English as a second language.
```

Figure 3.16

7. Repeat steps 1–6 to give a hanging indent to the Newcomers Saturday School paragraph.

> **Reminder**
> Now that you've used cascading menus, the numbered steps will be stated in more general terms, and will look like this: Choose Paragraph from the Layout menu, and then choose Hanging Indent.

EXIT If necessary, you can save your document, exit WordPerfect now, and continue this project later. Save your document as SERVICE2.DOC.

SETTING LINE SPACING

Line spacing is used to vary the white space between lines. The default in WordPerfect is single spacing, but you can easily change the line spacing using the Power Bar or the Line Spacing dialog box. You can use the Line Spacing button on the Power Bar to select single spacing, one and one-half spacing, or double spacing. Using the Line Spacing dialog box, you can set any spacing by typing a new space value from 0.1 to 160, or you can select values by scrolling through the line spacing values with the up and down scroll bar arrows or and .

The [Ln Spacing] code is inserted at the beginning of a paragraph and affects all the text from that point to the end of the document, unless you again change line spacing later in the document.

> **Tip**
> A useful technique to change line spacing for a specific block of text is to select the text and then choose the desired line spacing.

➤ **To change line spacing of a paragraph in the SERVICE.DOC document using the Power Bar:**

1. Toggle the Ruler Bar on.
2. Select the paragraph that begins *Are you.*
3. Press the Line Spacing button on the Power Bar.

The Line Spacing pull-down menu is displayed as shown in Figure 3.17.

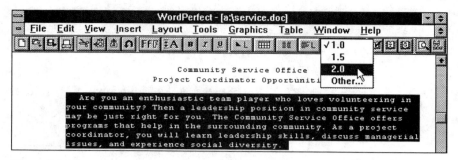

Figure 3.17

4. Select 2.0 for double spacing.

   Because you changed line spacing for a selected block of text, a [Ln Spacing:2.0] code is now inserted at the beginning of the paragraph, and a [Ln Spacing:1.0] code, the default line spacing, is inserted after the selected block. You can verify this with Reveal Codes.

➤ **To change line spacing of a paragraph using the Line Spacing dialog box:**

1. Select the paragraph that begins with *Below are some.*
2. Choose Line from the Layout menu, and then choose Spacing.

   The Line Spacing dialog box appears, as shown in Figure 3.18.
3. Type **2** in the Spacing text box to set double spacing.
4. Select OK.

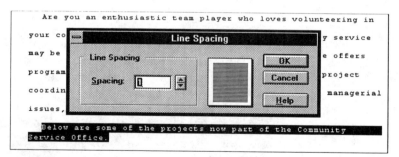

Figure 3.18

Forcing a New Page

A standard typing page in Canada is 8.5 by 11 inches, and text is usually printed six lines per inch, or 66 lines per page. The default top and bottom margins are 1 inch each, leaving only 9 inches or 54 lines per page on which to print. Depending on how you change the margins and the size of the printed characters, you can have more or less than 54 lines of text printed on a page. The status bar at the bottom of the screen keeps track of this information as you type.

When you reach the bottom of the page, a *soft page break* is automatically inserted in the document, and a single line is displayed across the screen. At this point you begin typing a new page.

In many writing situations, a soft page break occurs at an inconvenient place in the text. A page break may occur in the middle of a paragraph you do not want to see divided onto separate pages, or you may complete a section of a report and wish to start the next section on the next page. In these situations, you need to insert a *hard page break,* forcing text onto a new page. You will insert a hard page formatting code at the location you want the page break to occur by pressing [CTRL] + [ENTER] or by choosing Page Break from the Insert menu. A hard page break code displays a double line across the screen at that point in the document. If you insert or delete text, that page will always end at the hard page break. You delete a hard page break code as you do any other formatting code: by positioning the insertion point in front of the code and pressing [DEL].

➤ To insert a hard page break using the keyboard:

1. Place the insertion point at the beginning of the line *Literacy Projects*.
2. Press [CTRL] + [ENTER]

   A double line is displayed across the screen, and the status bar reads Pg 2 Ln 2".

➤ To delete a hard page break:

1. Toggle on Reveal Codes.
2. Place the insertion point in front of the [HPg] code.
3. Press [DEL]

➤ To insert a hard page break using the Insert menu:

1. Place the insertion point at the beginning of the line *Literacy Projects*.
2. Choose Page Break from the Insert menu, as shown in **Figure 3.19**.

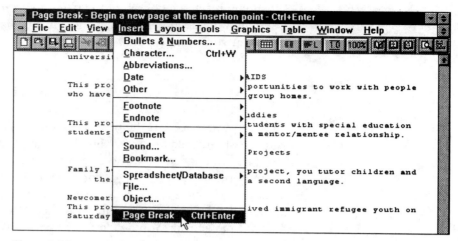

Figure 3.19

Check that a double line is displayed across the screen just above the heading *Literacy Projects*.

3. Save your edited document as SERVICE2.DOC.

The Next Step

This project introduced you to formatting techniques you can use to lay out text attractively on the page. The basic guideline was to use white space as a design element in the document. The formatting techniques discussed were setting margins, justifying text, setting tabs, indenting, varying line spacing, and forcing page breaks.

The formatting techniques you applied in this project should be used in other documents you will type. You should look at familiar documents and figure out how different formatting techniques were applied. Some examples are a book's table of contents, a restaurant menu, a program for a play, and the syllabus of a college course. Long documents such as class projects and research reports are more readable when they are written using variations in formatting.

You have successfully completed Project 3. You can either exit WordPerfect 6 for Windows or go on to work the Study Questions and Review Exercises.

Summary

- You use the formatting features of WordPerfect to arrange text attractively on the page.
- Reveal Codes lets you see the formatting codes embedded in a document.
- You can insert the desired formatting codes into the document with the Ruler Bar and dialog boxes.

- You can set unique margins for the whole document or for sections within a document. The Ruler Bar displays the current margin settings and can be used to easily change them.

- You can left-, center-, right-, or fully justify text between the left and right margins. The title of a document is often center justified.

- Tabs are useful for justifying text at different positions other than the left or right margin. The Ruler Bar displays the current tab settings and can be used to change any or all of them easily.

- When you indent paragraphs to align the text on a tab location, it serves as a temporary left margin.

- You can change line spacing and limit the number of lines printed on the page with a hard page break.

Key Terms and Operations

Key Terms
absolute tab
dot leaders
formatting
formatting code
hard page break
indenting
justification
line spacing
margin
margin marker
relative tab
Reveal Codes divider line
soft page break
subheading
tab marker
tab setting
white space

Operations
Center
Justification
Line
Line Spacing
Margins
Page
Page Break
Paragraph
Reveal Codes
Tab Set

Study Questions

MULTIPLE CHOICE

1. Formatting refers to:
   a. varying line spacing.
   b. indenting paragraphs.
   c. justifying text.
   d. changing margins.
   e. All of the above.

2. The main idea of formatting text is to:
   a. spell all the words correctly.
   b. put as much text on a page as possible.
   c. use the Ruler Bar whenever possible.
   d. arrange the text attractively.
   e. save files to disk.

3. A formatting code is set in the document:
   a. and cannot be deleted.
   b. at the location where you want the formatting effect to begin.
   c. by pressing ENTER.
   d. with the Ruler Bar.
   e. only at the very beginning of a page.

4. The Ruler Bar is composed of:
   a. margin markers.
   b. tab markers.
   c. a ruled line in 1/8-inch increments.
   d. All of the above.

5. The correct procedure to justify text of a particular paragraph is to:
   a. select the paragraph and then choose the desired justification.
   b. move the insertion point to the beginning of the page and then choose the desired justification.
   c. click the Line Spacing button on the Power Bar.
   d. turn on Reveal Codes.
   e. ask your friend.

6. What controls how far text is indented?
   a. Line spacing
   b. Hard page breaks
   c. Tabs
   d. Left justification
   e. Top and bottom margins

7. A left margin is set at 2 inches, and a relative tab is set at 1 inch to the right of the left margin. What is the equivalent absolute tab setting for the same tab?
   a. 1 inch
   b. 2 inches
   c. 3 inches
   d. 4 inches
   e. There is no equivalent setting.

8. The most common layout used for the title of a document is:
   a. a soft page break.
   b. center-justified.
   c. triple-spaced.
   d. hanging indent.
   e. Reveal Codes.

9. The Tab Set button on the Power Bar is used to insert a:
   a. margin code.
   b. paragraph format code.
   c. on/off toggle code.
   d. justification code.
   e. None of the above.

10. TAB is used to:
    a. force a page break.
    b. indent a paragraph.
    c. set new tabs.
    d. change line spacing.
    e. justify text between the left and right margins.

SHORT ANSWER

1. Why is Reveal Codes a useful feature?
2. How do you use the Ruler Bar to change margins and tabs?
3. Why would you use a dialog box rather than the Ruler Bar or Power Bar to change margins, tabs, or line spacing?
4. What are different formatting techniques to create white space around text in a document?
5. Why is it important to place the insertion point at the desired location in the document before inserting a formatting code?

REVIEW EXERCISES

Review the concepts presented in Project 3 by completing the following.

Developing a Class Handout

You have read a number of articles in your communications class about the importance of making meetings more productive. You have identified ten guidelines to encourage participation and increase interaction of people attending meetings. You are now preparing a presentation on this material and need to type a handout for the class.

1. Give the handout a good title, and make sure that the ten tips for a good meeting stand out clearly, as shown in Figure 3.20.
2. Use different text layouts. Examples are to center the subheadings and double indent the paragraphs.
3. Experiment with hanging indents.
4. Save the document as MEETING.DOC.
5. Close the document.

    You will use this document in Project 4.

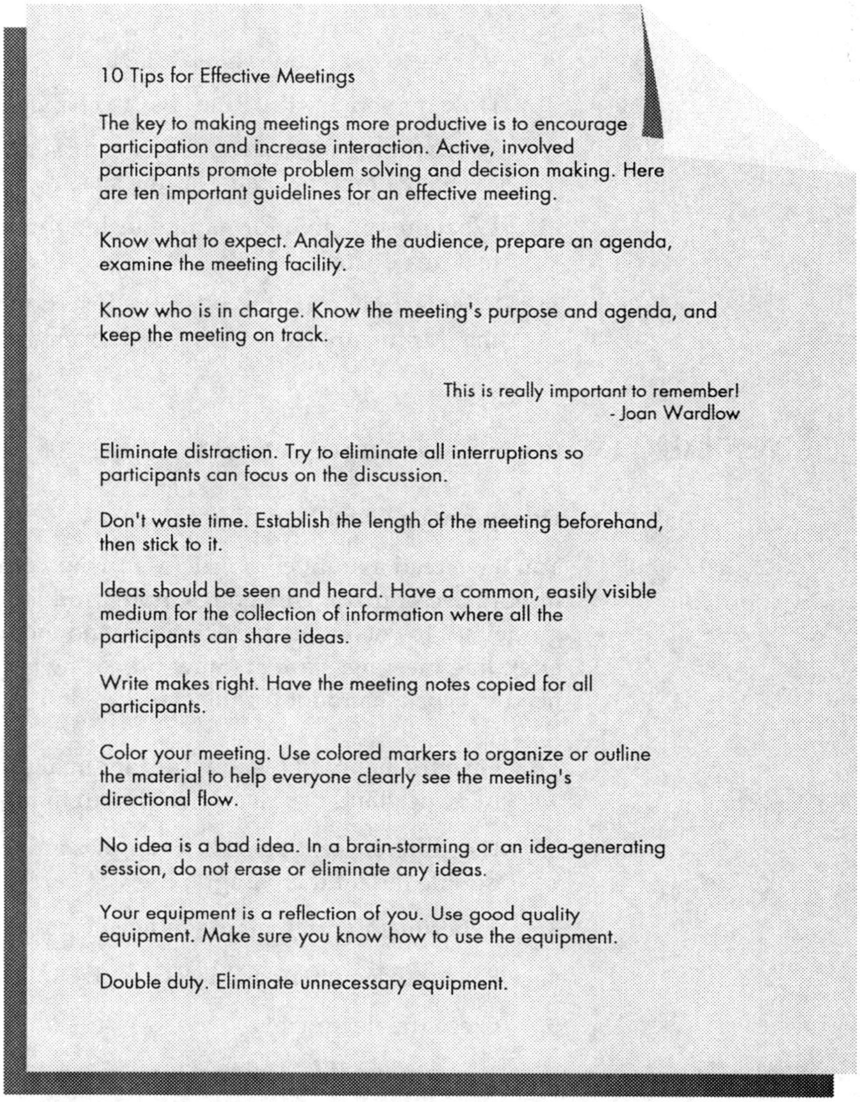

10 Tips for Effective Meetings

The key to making meetings more productive is to encourage participation and increase interaction. Active, involved participants promote problem solving and decision making. Here are ten important guidelines for an effective meeting.

Know what to expect. Analyze the audience, prepare an agenda, examine the meeting facility.

Know who is in charge. Know the meeting's purpose and agenda, and keep the meeting on track.

> This is really important to remember!
> - Joan Wardlow

Eliminate distraction. Try to eliminate all interruptions so participants can focus on the discussion.

Don't waste time. Establish the length of the meeting beforehand, then stick to it.

Ideas should be seen and heard. Have a common, easily visible medium for the collection of information where all the participants can share ideas.

Write makes right. Have the meeting notes copied for all participants.

Color your meeting. Use colored markers to organize or outline the material to help everyone clearly see the meeting's directional flow.

No idea is a bad idea. In a brain-storming or an idea-generating session, do not erase or eliminate any ideas.

Your equipment is a reflection of you. Use good quality equipment. Make sure you know how to use the equipment.

Double duty. Eliminate unnecessary equipment.

Figure 3.20

Competency Testing

- Review the Topic Objectives to ensure you have mastered all skills listed.
- Check off:
  - Your completed Project work (the file SERVICE2.DOC).
  - Your completed Multiple Choice exercises.
  - Your completed Review Exercises (the file MEETING.DOC and your TDL).
- Examine the **Formatting the Document**:
  - **Project Sample Sheet** to compare your work against the sample.
  - **Multiple Choice Correct Answer Sheet** to compare your answers against the correct ones.
  - **Review Exercises Sample Answer Sheet** to compare your work against it.

Enhancing the Document

Topic Objectives

After completing this topic, you should be able to:

- Change the typeface and type size.
- Emphasize text with boldface, underlining, and italics.
- Enter special characters (*Note:* Covered in Practice Exercises *only*).
- Position page numbers.
- Add headers and footers.
- Add footnotes and endnotes (*Note:* Covered in Practice Exercises *only*).

Computer Tutorial

- Work through:

2.2	Using the Power Bar (review changing the typeface and type size, if necessary; done in the **Introduction to WordPerfect 6 for Windows** topic)
3.4.1	Fonts and Type Styles
3.5.2	Headers and Footers
3.5.3	Page Views and Layout

Practice Exercises

- Read and complete all **Project 4 work** outlined on pages 93 to 107:
    - Take special note of the **Summary** and **Key Terms and Operations** sections.
    - Make sure to save the file **MEETING2.DOC** as indicated on page 106. Be careful to use the "Save As" operation when you save this file so that you don't overwrite the original file created in the review exercises of the last topic.
- Do **Multiple Choice** exercises on pages 107 and 108.
- Do all **Review Exercises** on page 109, making sure to save the file **QUESTION.DOC**.
- Do the required **Topic Directory Listing** (TDL).

PROJECT 4: ENHANCING THE DOCUMENT

CASE STUDY: ENHANCING A CLASS HANDOUT

In Project 3, you learned how to format, or attractively arrange, the text on the page to improve the readability of the document. Using WordPerfect 6 for Windows, you can further enhance the readability of a document. For example, you can change the visual characteristics of the text on the printed page to emphasize important ideas and convey an overall feel for the intent of the document. You can also provide additional text on the page that orients readers to where they are reading in the document and to supplemental information that supports the main ideas in the text.

A guiding principle for enhancing a document is to design its appearance so that readers will be more likely to understand and use the information. You want both to communicate your ideas clearly and to make your message understandable and functional. The visual appeal of a document is an important factor in how readers both interpret the author's meaning or intent and use the document later as a source of information for their own purposes.

For this fourth project, assume you have been asked by your revered professor to enhance your class handout on the topic of making meetings more productive. You typed the draft of this document in the Review Exercises in Project 3 and saved it as MEETING.DOC. You read a magazine article about productive meetings and need to cite it in the handout. You also want to add visual emphasis to the title and the ten guidelines. You want to footnote a reference in the document that inspired the report and a quotation from a person you interviewed. Since you anticipate that the document will be expanded into a term paper later in the course, you might as well include pagination and a header.

DESIGNING THE SOLUTION

You can enhance the readability of a document by changing the appearance of the printed text and by orienting the reader to useful supplementary information. A number of design techniques are available for you to do this.

Changing the Appearance of Text

You can visually enhance text by changing the font used to print the text. A *font* has three characteristics: *typeface*, *type style*, and *type size*.

The term *typeface* refers to the design and shape of a set of characters. Many typefaces are available, including the popular Courier, Helvetica, and Times Roman. A *serif typeface* has small cross lines, or serifs, at the end strokes of each letter; the serifs are not included in a *sans serif typeface.* A serif typeface, such as Courier or Times Roman, is easy on the eye and provides a more formal, authoritative look to a document. The more simple-looking characters in a sans serif typeface, such as Helvetica or Universal, convey a more informal, laid-back feel. Serif typefaces are often used for the text of longer documents, such as books and research reports, whereas sans serif typefaces are generally used in shorter documents, such as logos and announcements, and for titles and headings to provide a visual contrast from the main body of the text.

Type style is the special visual characteristics or attributes of important words or phrases in the text. Frequently used type styles are boldface, italics, underlining, and superscripting. Boldface is usually used to emphasize titles or subheadings, whereas underlining is used more often to emphasize words or phrases in the text. Italics is also used for emphasis and for foreign words and long block quotes. A *superscript* is a character positioned slightly above other characters on the same line. Superscripts are used for displaying footnote or endnote numbers, as well as for trademark symbols and exponents.

The term *type size* refers to the vertical measurement of characters. Type is measured in points, with 1 point equal to 1/72 inch. Typical type sizes for documents of any serious length are 10 and 12 points, although in newspaper columns the type may be as small as 8 points. Type sizes larger than 14 points usually are not used for large amounts of text. The larger the type size, the fewer the characters that can be printed on a line. An accepted guideline is that a line of text should have 45 to 65 characters. Thus, you need to consider widening the left and right margins when you increase the type size and narrowing the margins when you decrease the type size.

You can vary the three font characteristics in interesting and effective ways. However, you should follow a few helpful guidelines:

- Choose a typeface appropriate for the document. For example, use a more conventional typeface for term papers but something unusual and interesting for announcements or advertisements.

- Use no more than two typefaces in a document: serif for text and sans serif for titles, headings, and subheads. Vary the type size to indicate the hierarchy of elements and levels of subheads.

- Use variations of type style judiciously. Too much boldface, underlining, or italics can easily result in a visually confusing document.

Including Supplementary Information to Orient Readers

You can orient readers to various parts of your text by using page numbering, *headers* and *footers*, and *footnotes* and *endnotes*.

Page numbering helps readers keep track of where they are sequentially in a document, especially in long documents. Pagination is also useful in finding a particular section of the document when it is referred to later.

Headers and *footers* are blocks of text printed at the top and bottom of each page, respectively. Typical headers and footers include the report and chapter titles, but you can include any useful text in headers and footers. For example, your term papers could include your name, the title of the paper, and the course number at the bottom of each page. The current date also is often displayed in a header or footer. Headers and footers are very effective in reminding readers where and what they are reading.

Footnotes and *endnotes* are references, explanations, or comments placed outside the regular text. They are used to cite the sources for ideas or quotations and for adding supplementary comments to the text. They are frequently used in term papers, research reports, business reports, and books.

Figure 4.1 shows the MEETING.DOC document with the enhancements you will be working on in this project. Open the MEETING.DOC file now to continue with this project.

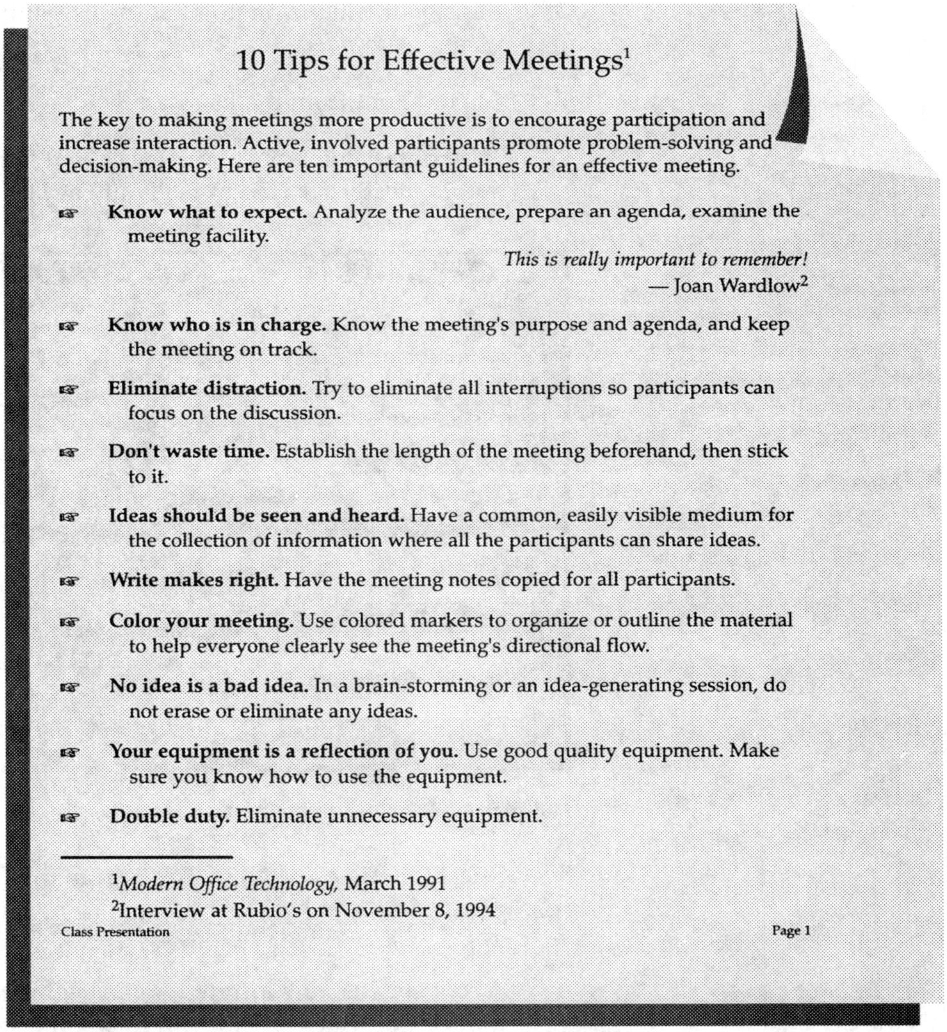

10 Tips for Effective Meetings[1]

The key to making meetings more productive is to encourage participation and increase interaction. Active, involved participants promote problem-solving and decision-making. Here are ten important guidelines for an effective meeting.

- **Know what to expect.** Analyze the audience, prepare an agenda, examine the meeting facility.

    This is really important to remember!
    — Joan Wardlow[2]

- **Know who is in charge.** Know the meeting's purpose and agenda, and keep the meeting on track.

- **Eliminate distraction.** Try to eliminate all interruptions so participants can focus on the discussion.

- **Don't waste time.** Establish the length of the meeting beforehand, then stick to it.

- **Ideas should be seen and heard.** Have a common, easily visible medium for the collection of information where all the participants can share ideas.

- **Write makes right.** Have the meeting notes copied for all participants.

- **Color your meeting.** Use colored markers to organize or outline the material to help everyone clearly see the meeting's directional flow.

- **No idea is a bad idea.** In a brain-storming or an idea-generating session, do not erase or eliminate any ideas.

- **Your equipment is a reflection of you.** Use good quality equipment. Make sure you know how to use the equipment.

- **Double duty.** Eliminate unnecessary equipment.

---
[1]*Modern Office Technology*, March 1991
[2]Interview at Rubio's on November 8, 1994

Class Presentation   Page 1

Figure 4.1

CHANGING TYPEFACE AND TYPE SIZE

Changing the typeface and size can dramatically affect the impact of your text. Since you are using the MEETING.DOC document as a handout and possibly as an overhead for a presentation, the typeface should provide an authoritative feel without undue formality. Increasing the type size of the title and headings would draw the reader's attention to those important information items.

You can select the three font characteristics—typeface, type size, and type style—using the Font option from the Layout menu. The font selection available on your computer depends on the type of printer you are using. In this project, if you are directed to use a typeface not in the dialog box, you can select an appropriate available alternative.

➤ To change the typeface:

1. Position the insertion point at the beginning of the MEETING.DOC document.

2. Choose Font from the Layout menu.

    The Font dialog box appears as shown in Figure 4.2. The default typeface, automatically selected in the Font Face list box, is probably Courier New.

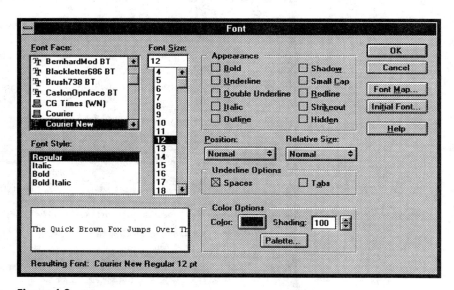

Figure 4.2

3. Select CG Times (WN) or Times from the Font Face list box.

4. Select 12 from the Font Size list box, and then select OK.

    A font code is now inserted at the beginning of the document. This *base font* of CG Times typeface and 12-point type size will be used to print text to the end of the document, unless you change the font later. You can change the typeface using the Font dialog box or the Font Face button on the Power Bar.

You can change type size using either the Font Size list box in the Font dialog box, the Relative Size drop-down list in the Font dialog box, or the Font Size button on the Power Bar. Each time you select Large from the Relative Size drop-down list, the base font is increased 20 percent; this is equivalent to selecting 14 as the point size when the base font is 12. You can choose Extra Large to make the point size twice as large, which is equivalent to having 24-point type in comparison to a 12-point base font.

➤ **To change the type size of the title using the Font dialog box:**

1. Select the block of text comprising the title, *10 Tips for Effective Meetings*.
2. Choose Font from the Layout menu.
3. Select Extra Large from the Relative Size drop-down list.
4. Select OK.

➤ **To change the type size of a heading using the Font Size button on the Power Bar:**

1. Select the block of text comprising the second heading, *Know what to expect*.

2. Click the Font Size button on the Power Bar, and then select 14 from the drop-down list.

Go through the document and change the size of the other headings using the method you prefer.

BOLDFACING, UNDERLINING, AND ITALICIZING TEXT

You can change the style or appearance of text using either the Appearance check box group in the Font dialog box or the font style buttons on the Power Bar. The reason for changing the text appearance is to emphasize the importance of the text. Remember not to overuse style changes; doing so can easily lead to a visually confusing document.

➤ **To boldface a heading using the Font dialog box:**

1. Select the block of text comprising the first heading, *Know what to expect*.
2. Choose Font from the Layout menu.

    The Font dialog box appears, as shown in Figure 4.2.

3. Select the Bold check box from the Appearance group.
4. Select OK.

Italicizing, underlining, and other style changes can be made in the same way using the Font dialog box. You can also use the Power Bar.

➤ To italicize a quote using the Power Bar:

1. Select the block of text, *This is really important to remember!*

2. Click the Italic Font button on the Power Bar.

You can apply boldfacing and underlining in the same way using the Bold Font and Underline Font buttons on the Power Bar.

Go through the document and boldface the remaining headings using the method that is most convenient for you.

> **Tip**
> You can also press CTRL+B to boldface, CTRL+I to italicize, and CTRL+U to underline.

Using Special Character Sets

What do you do when you want to type a character that is not on the keyboard? The character you need is probably in one of the 14 sets of special characters available in WordPerfect, including scientific, mathematical, typographical, iconic, Greek, Hebrew, and Japanese. WordPerfect 6 has more than 1500 characters from which you can choose. This feature is especially useful considering today's increased emphasis on cultural diversity and international business. You can access special character sets through the Insert menu.

➤ To insert a special character:

1. Position the insertion point at the beginning of the first heading, *Know what to expect.*

   Verify with Reveal Codes that the insertion point is positioned before the style and size codes.

2. Choose Character from the Insert menu.

   The WordPerfect Characters dialog box appears, as shown in Figure 4.3.

Enhancing the Document

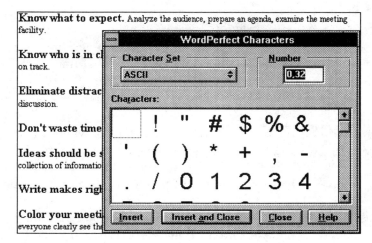

Figure 4.3

3. Select Iconic Symbols from the Character Set drop-down list.

4. Select the hand pointer icon.

   The symbol is surrounded with a flashing dotted line when you select it, as shown in Figure 4.4.

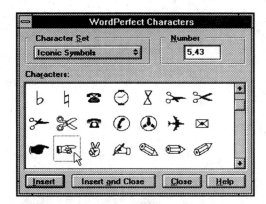

Figure 4.4

5. Select the Insert button to insert the character in the document.

   The WordPerfect Characters dialog box remains on the screen. If you need to select only one character, you can select the Insert and Close button. You can insert only one character at a time.

6. Go through the document and insert other special characters to jazz up the headings.

7. Select Close when you are finished inserting special characters.

> **Reminder**
> You can see how the document will look on the printed page by using the Zoom button on the Power Bar.

NUMBERING PAGES

A convenient way to keep track of where you are reading in a document is to glance at the page number. For a one- or two-page document, such as MEETING.DOC, you may decide that page numbering is not necessary. However, for longer documents, page numbering is essential.

WordPerfect keeps track of page numbers automatically and displays the current page number on the status bar. WordPerfect does not print page numbers on your document, however, unless you insert the appropriate page-numbering format code in the document. You insert the page-numbering code on the page you want to begin printing page numbers. If you had a research paper with a table of contents and an introduction, you could paginate those pages with Roman numerals; you could then insert another code on the first page of the remainder of the document to paginate with Arabic numerals. You will use the Page Numbering dialog box to control the position of the page number on the page and the page number's appearance.

➤ **To position and add text to the page numbers:**

1. Position the insertion point at the beginning of the MEETING.DOC document.

2. Choose Page from the Layout menu, and then choose Numbering.

   The Page Numbering dialog box appears as shown in Figure 4.5.

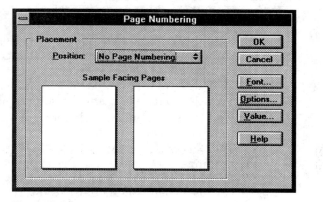

Figure 4.5

3. Select Bottom Right from the Position drop-down list.

   The page number is displayed in the selected position in the Sample Facing Pages preview windows.

4. Select Options.

   The Page Numbering Options dialog box appears as shown in Figure 4.6.

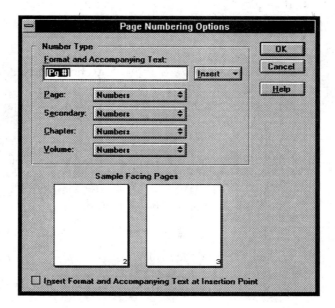

Figure 4.6

5. Position the insertion point at the very beginning of the Format and Accompanying Text text box, before the [Pg#] symbol.

   The [Pg#] symbol in the text box controls the printing of the actual page number. Make sure you don't erase this symbol.

6. Type **Page** and press [SPACE]

   The new appearance for the page numbers is displayed in the Sample Facing Pages preview windows. You can experiment with different combinations of positions and accompanying text.

7. When you have decided what you like, select OK to return to the Page Numbering dialog box.

8. Select OK to close the Page Numbering dialog box.

EXIT If necessary, you can save your document, exit WordPerfect now, and continue this project later. Save the document as MEETING2.DOC.

Adding Headers and Footers

A header and a footer provide information about the document and are printed at the top and bottom of a page, respectively. Whether to use headers or footers, and exactly what type of information should be placed in them, usually depends on the purpose of the document and the writing guidelines you are following. Typical information in a header or footer are the title, a heading, or the current date.

You create headers and footers by choosing Header/Footer from the Layout menu. You type and edit headers and footers in an identical manner, and you can include anything you want in them, even page numbers. You can have as many as two headers and two footers. A header or footer is printed beginning on the page where it was created. They can appear on every page or just even-numbered or odd-numbered pages. You can suppress printing them on pages in the document where you decide they are not needed. You can view headers and footers displayed on-screen, and you should verify that they are not overlapping each other or the page numbers.

➤ **To enter footer information:**

1. Position the insertion point at the beginning of the MEETING.DOC document.

2. Choose Page from the View menu.

3. Choose Header/Footer from the Layout menu.

    The Headers/Footers dialog box appears as shown in Figure 4.7.

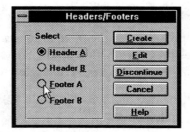

Figure 4.7

4. Select Footer A, and then select Create.

    The Header/Footer Feature Bar is displayed just below the Power Bar, and the insertion point is located at the bottom of the page, where you will type the footer, as shown in Figure 4.8.

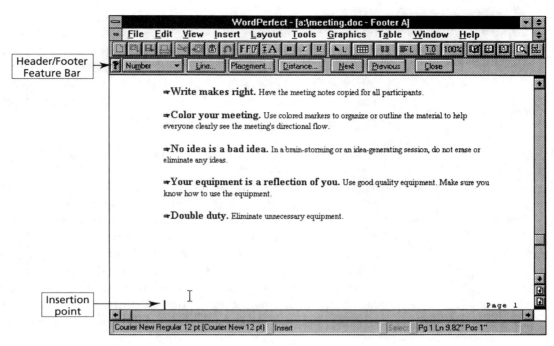

Figure 4.8

5. Type **Class Presentation**

6. Select Close on the Header/Footer Feature Bar to clear it from the document window.

   You can verify that the footer was inserted correctly with Reveal Codes. Use Zoom to see how the page will look with the footer. You can use the Header/Footer Feature Bar to edit an existing header or footer.

➤ To change the typeface of a footer:

1. Position the insertion point at the beginning of the MEETING.DOC document.

2. Choose Header/Footer from the Layout menu.

3. Select Footer A, and then select Edit.

   The insertion point is placed at the beginning of the text of Footer A at the bottom of the page.

4. Select the text *Class Presentation.*

5. Click the Font Face button on the Power Bar and then select CG Times (WN) or Times from the drop-down list.

6. Select Close on the Header/Footer Feature Bar.

Adding Footnotes and Endnotes

Footnotes and endnotes supplement information in a document or provide references to other sources of information. Footnotes are placed at the bottom of the page; endnotes are grouped at the end of the document. Whether to use footnotes or endnotes, and exactly what type of information should be placed in footnotes or endnotes, usually depends on the purpose of the document and the writing guidelines you are following.

Footnotes and endnotes are numbered or lettered sequentially. If you use both in one document, you can number footnotes and letter endnotes, or vice versa. The footnote and endnote numbers and letters are displayed as superscripts next to the text being referenced. WordPerfect automatically adjusts the number of lines of text on the page when footnotes are added. If you insert a new footnote or endnote before existing notes, WordPerfect automatically renumbers the notes. Also, if you move footnoted text to another page, the footnote is also moved to that page. Other footnotes affected by inserting new notes or moving notes are automatically repositioned and renumbered. Endnotes are printed after a hard page break at the end of the document or at the end of a particular section of the document, depending on what you specify.

Typing and editing footnotes and endnotes are identical processes, except for the placement of the notes. You use Footnote and Endnote in the Insert menu.

➤ **To create a footnote attached to the name Joan Wardlow:**

1. Position the insertion point just after the name *Joan Wardlow.*

2. Choose Footnote from the Insert menu, and then choose Create.

    The Footnote/Endnote Feature Bar is displayed just below the Power Bar and the footnote number and insertion point are located at the bottom of the page, where you will type the footnote, as shown in Figure 4.9.

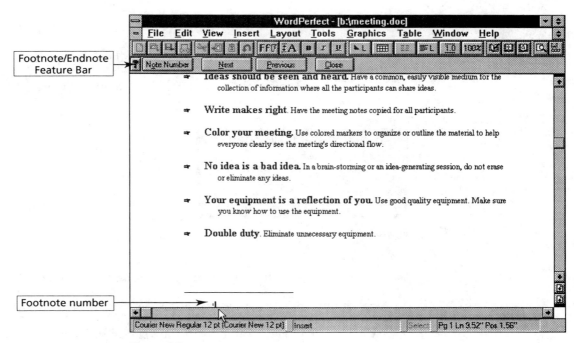

Figure 4.9

3. Type **Interview at Rubio's, November 8, 1994**

4. Select Close on the Footnote/Endnote Feature Bar.

   You can verify that the footnote was inserted correctly with Reveal Codes and by using Zoom to see how the page will look with the footnote.

➤ To create a footnote before the previous one:

1. Position the insertion point at the very end of the title *10 Tips for Effective Meetings*.

2. Choose Footnote from the Insert menu, and then choose Create.

   The Footnote/Endnote Feature Bar is displayed and the footnote number and insertion point are placed at the bottom of the page for typing the new footnote. Notice that WordPerfect has already changed the number of the footnote associated with the name Joan Wardlow.

3. Type **Modern Office Technology, March 1991**

4. Select the text *Modern Office Technology*.

5. Click the Italic Font button on the Power Bar.

6. Select Close on the Footnote/Endnote Feature Bar.

   You can verify the placement and numbering of the footnotes by looking at the document using Reveal Codes or the Zoom feature. You can use the Footnote/Endnote Feature Bar to edit an existing footnote or endnote.

➤ **To change the typeface of an existing footnote:**

1. Choose Footnote from the Insert menu, and then choose Edit.

   The Edit Footnote dialog box appears as shown in Figure 4.10.

Figure 4.10

2. Type **2** in the Footnote Number text box, and then select OK.

3. Select the footnote text *Interview at Rubio's, November 8, 1994*.

4. Click the Font Face button on the Power Bar and then select CG Times (WN) or Times from the drop-down list.

5. Select Close on the Footnote/Endnote Feature Bar.

6. Save and close your document as MEETING2.DOC.

You can use Zoom to see how the document will look when you print it. You did it. Another good effort, and another project accomplished.

THE NEXT STEP

This project introduced you to document-enhancing techniques you can use to attract readers' attention to important ideas in the document and to orient readers to what and where they are reading in the document. The enhancing techniques discussed were changing font characteristics, such as typeface, type size, and type style; using special characters; page numbering; using footers and headers; and using footnotes and endnotes.

You have probably thought of variations on these document enhancements to emphasize text and orient the readers' attention. If you have a color printer, you can use the Color Options group in the Font dialog box to vary text color. You can familiarize yourself with the special character sets. Footnote and endnote numbers are automatically superscripted, but you can type simple expressions or formulas such as H_2O and $E=mc^2$ by using Subscript and Superscript in the position drop-down list in the Font dialog box.

This concludes Project 4. You can either exit WordPerfect 6 for Windows or go on to work the Study Questions and Review Exercises.

Summary

- You use enhancing techniques to attract readers' attention to important ideas and to orient them to the appropriate location in the document.
- Changing the typeface and type size of the text can dramatically affect the readers' ability to read and remember important ideas in the document.
- Using boldface, underlining, and italics is effective for limited amounts of text.
- There are many special characters not on the keyboard that you can insert into documents.
- When you begin typing longer documents, you need to consider using page numbering and headers or footers.
- Footnotes and endnotes are appropriate for citing sources of information and supplementary material to the main text.

Key Terms and Operations

Key Terms
base font
endnote
font
footer
footnote
header
sans serif typeface
serif typeface
superscript
typeface
type size
type style

Operations
Endnote
Font
Footers
Footnote
Headers
Page Numbering

Study Questions

MULTIPLE CHOICE

1. The overall design and shape of a set of characters is called:
   a. type style.
   b. page number.
   c. superscript.
   d. typeface.
   e. boldface.

2. Type style refers to:
   a. the position of the text on the page.
   b. the appearance of the text.
   c. the height of each character.
   d. headers and footers.
   e. footnotes.

3. If you want to type a symbol but cannot find it on the keyboard, you probably will find it in:
   a. the Thesaurus.
   b. the Help Glossary.
   c. the Layout menu.
   d. one of the special character sets.
   e. the Ruler.

4. The vertical height of characters is measured in:
   a. tabs.
   b. spaces.
   c. points.
   d. lines.
   e. headers.

5. If you want to acknowledge someone's special contribution of an idea in your document, you use a:
   a. title or heading.
   b. footnote or endnote.
   c. page number.
   d. header or footer.
   e. different typeface.

6. Typefaces can be differentiated by whether they are:
   a. serif or sans serif.
   b. big or small.
   c. boldfaced or italicized.
   d. special characters or not.
   e. underlined or superscripted.

7. To emphasize the title and headings of a document, you can:
   a. print them as footnotes or endnotes.
   b. increase their type size.
   c. decrease their type size.
   d. narrow the margins.
   e. use a different typeface for each word.

8. Which of the following is a useful guideline for font selection?
   a. Use as much underlining as possible.
   b. Alternate between serif and sans serif typefaces.
   c. Choose a typeface appropriate for the document.
   d. Select at least a 16-point size for the text.
   e. All of the above.

9. To print more large-sized characters on a line, you need to:
   a. narrow the left and right margins.
   b. select a serif typeface.
   c. use subscripts.
   d. widen the left and right margins.
   e. increase the top margin.

10. The WordPerfect Characters dialog box provides:
    a. access to characters not on the keyboard.
    b. more than 1500 special characters.
    c. language and scientific characters.
    d. icons and line-drawing characters.
    e. All of the above.

SHORT ANSWER

1. How might you unintentionally create a cluttered-looking document that distracts readers?
2. What are some useful guidelines for using document-enhancing techniques?
3. What types of information should be placed in a footer or header? What types of information should be placed in footnotes or endnotes?
4. Where in the Help feature would you look for information about fonts?
5. Why should you paginate documents? How do you decide where to place page numbers?

REVIEW EXERCISES

Review the concepts presented in Project 4 by completing the following.

Developing a Questionnaire

You have been asked to design a short questionnaire to collect information from European companies about the impact of the European Community on their advertising plans. The questionnaire should contain easily understood questions; a simple, straightforward way to answer; and clear instructions. The initial design of the questionnaire is shown in Figure 4.11. Use the Iconic Symbols character set to locate the check box used in the questionnaire. Vary the use of boldface and italics. Save the document as QUESTION.DOC.

EUROPEAN COMMUNITY SURVEY

1. What is the primary line of business of your firm? ________________
2. Where is the corporate headquarters of your firm? (check one)
   ❐ US ❐ Japan ❐ Germany ❐ France
   ❐ Italy ❐ UK ❐ Other ________________
3. Currently, which of the following is your firm's most important European Community market? (check one)
   ❐ Germany ❐ France ❐ Italy ❐ UK ❐ Other ________________

The following questions are scaled as follows:

EL = Extremely likely this will occur
VL = Very likely this will occur
SL = Somewhat likely this will occur
NL = Not very likely this will occur
DK = Don't know whether this will occur

As a result of plans for political and economic cooperation in Europe, how likely are the following consequences?

	EL	VL	SL	NL	DK
1. Advertising expenditures as a percentage of sales will decrease.	❐	❐	❐	❐	❐
2. Advertising will be more strictly regulated.	❐	❐	❐	❐	❐
3. Television advertising will become more widely used.	❐	❐	❐	❐	❐
4. Standardized European advertising media will increase.	❐	❐	❐	❐	❐
5. There will be an increase of TV advertising dubbed in the local language.	❐	❐	❐	❐	❐
6. Advertising will be based more on similarity of values rather than on national or cultural identity.	❐	❐	❐	❐	❐

Figure 4.11

COMPETENCY TESTING

- Review the Topic Objectives to ensure you have mastered all skills listed.
- Check off:
  - Your completed Project work (the file MEETING2.DOC).
  - Your completed Multiple Choice exercises.
  - Your completed Review Exercises (the file QUESTION.DOC and your TDL).
- Examine the **Enhancing the Document**:
  - **Project Sample Sheet** to compare your work against the sample.
  - **Multiple Choice Correct Answer Sheet** to compare your answers against the correct ones.
  - **Review Exercises Sample Answer Sheet** to compare your work against it.

Competency Test Preparation and Summary

Competency Test Preparation

Congratulations! You have now completed all the work in the *BASIS* Computer Applications WordPerfect 6 for Windows module. All you have to do now is:

- Review the objectives for all topics to ensure you have mastered all the skills for the module.
- Review your notes and practice where necessary.
- Check to make sure you have completed all work necessary to qualify you to attempt the competency test.
- Do the competency test.

Module Objectives

Here is a summary of the objectives for all topics in the module, in alphabetical order:

- Add headers and footers.
- Add footnotes and endnotes (*Note:* Covered in Practice Exercises *only*).
- Change the typeface and type size.
- Copy, delete, and move selected blocks of text within a document.
- Correct simple mistakes.
- Describe the components of a WordPerfect 6 for Windows document window.
- Differentiate between basic and advanced word processing features (*Note:* Covered in Practice Exercises *only*).
- Emphasize text with boldface, underlining, and italics.
- Enter special characters (*Note:* Covered in Practice Exercises *only*).
- Enter text into a document.
- Exit a document.
- Exit WordPerfect (*Note:* Covered in Practice Exercises *only*).
- Find text in a document.
- Indent paragraphs (*Note:* Covered in Practice Exercises *only*).
- Insert page breaks (*Note:* Covered in Practice Exercises *only*).

- Justify text.
- Lay out the design of a WordPerfect document (*Note:* Covered in Practice Exercises *only*).
- Move the insertion point around in a document.
- Name a document.
- Position page numbers.
- Preview a document (*Note:* Covered in Practice Exercises *only*).
- Print a document.
- Replace occurrences of specific text.
- Retrieve a document file from disk.
- Reveal formatting codes.
- Save a document to disk.
- Save a document under a different name.
- Set line spacing.
- Set margins.
- Set tabs (*Note:* Covered in Practice Exercises *only*).
- Start WordPerfect 6 for Windows.
- Use the Help feature (*Note:* Covered in Practice Exercises *only*).
- Use the Power Bar and the Button Bar.
- Use the WordPerfect Speller.
- Use the WordPerfect Thesaurus.
- Work with menus and dialog boxes using a mouse or the keyboard.

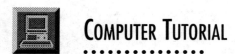

Computer Tutorial

If necessary, glance through computer tutorials. The **Summary** and **Quiz** sections at the end of tutorials are a good review.

Competency Testing

To qualify for the WordPerfect 6 for Windows module competency test, you must have completed all the work outlined in the Practice Exercises sections of each topic in the module, and have had all of that work checked off as summarized in the Competency Testing sections. For more information about module competency tests, consult your *BASIS* System Administrator and/or your *BASIS* User's Guide.

Double-check now to make sure that you have all work completed and checked off:

TOPIC	REQUIRED WORK
Introduction to WordPerfect 6 for Windows	❐ Multiple Choice Exercises
Creating a Document	❐ Project work (SEQUOIA.LTR) ❐ Multiple Choice Exercises ❐ Review Exercises work (SHERMAN.DOC and your TDL)
Editing the Document	❐ Project work (SHERMAN2.DOC) ❐ Multiple Choice Exercises ❐ Review Exercises work (SERVICE.DOC and your TDL)
Formatting the Document	❐ Project work (SERVICE2.DOC) ❐ Multiple Choice Exercises ❐ Review Exercises work (MEETING.DOC and your TDL)
Enhancing the Document	❐ Project work (MEETING2.DOC) ❐ Multiple Choice Exercises ❐ Review Exercises work (QUESTION.DOC and your TDL)

Summary

We hope that you have enjoyed your *BASIS* Computer Applications WordPerfect 6 for Windows module. This text will serve as a useful reference for you in the future, and the computer tutorials are often helpful for a quick review.

To further develop your WordPerfect skills, we highly recommend the following material from the computer tutorials listed below. (*Note:* The following is *not* required for the *BASIS* WordPerfect module competency test.)

SECTION	NOTES
5.1 Graphics	WordPerfect allows you to create a variety of graphics elements ranging from simple lines to elaborate figures. This tutorial shows you how to import figures from the clip art files included with your WordPerfect, and then how to place and size them to maximize the visual interest the incorporation of graphics provides.
5.2 Tables	A WordPerfect table stores data in columns and rows. There are distinct advantages to using tables as opposed to tabs and indents to align text in columns. The lines between data items improve readability. You can align text within cells and join cells. You can also perform calculations by entering formulas that act on numbers in the table.

In addition, we recommend that you learn how to work with multiple documents: don't retype text you have already typed and saved. The trick is to copy or move text.

There are four basic writing techniques you can use when working with multiple documents: the first is to view the text in one or more documents that serve(s) as a reminder or guide for what you should be writing in another document window. The second is to copy or move blocks of text from one document and insert them into one or more other documents. The third technique is to save a block of text from one document as a new, separate document, and the fourth is to retrieve a document and insert it into another document. The table that follows summarizes some of these strategies for your convenience. (*Note:* Once again, this material is *not* required for the *BASIS* WordPerfect module competency test.)

COMPETENCY TEST PREPARATION AND SUMMARY

OPERATION	FOLLOW THESE STEPS
Opening, Viewing, and Exiting Multiple Documents	You can have as many as nine documents open at one time. You can resize and arrange document windows using the same techniques you may have already used with the Windows Program Manager. You can move from one document window to another in three ways: (1) by selecting the appropriate document from the Window drop-down menu, (2) by moving the pointer and clicking the desired window if it is displayed on the screen, or (3) by using the keystroke combination [CTRL] + [F6]. As you work with the multiple documents, you should use the Save or Save As command as appropriate for each document. To open more than one document, simply choose Open from the File menu, select a document, choose Open again for the second document window, and so on. When you're done, exit each document in turn (in any order you prefer).
Copying and Moving Text Between Two Documents	The procedure for copying or moving text between documents is essentially the same as copying or moving text within the same document. The source and target files must be open first (as above); then you can select the text in the source document and copy or move it to the target document.
Saving Text from a Document to a New Document	If you anticipate reusing a block of text, you can save the block as a separate document that can later be retrieved, edited if necessary, and inserted into other documents. The procedure is to have the source document open, select the desired block of text, and use the Save As command to create a document containing only the text block. The block is not deleted from the source document.
Inserting a Document into Another Document	*Boilerplate* applications retrieve one or more source documents and insert them at desired locations in a target document. The procedure is to have the target document open, position the insertion point at the desired location, and use the File command from the Insert menu to copy the desired source document from disk and insert it. You can insert any number of source documents into one target document.

Operations Reference

Keystroke Combinations
Help

KEYBOARD	EXPLANATION
F1	Accesses Help.
SHFT + F1	Accesses context-sensitive Help.

Insertion-Point Movement

KEYBOARD	EXPLANATION
→	One character to the right.
←	One character to the left.
CTRL + →	One word to the right.
CTRL + ←	One word to the left.
END	End of the line.
HOME	Beginning of the line.
↑	One line up.
↓	One line down.
CTRL + ↑	Beginning of preceding paragraph.
CTRL + ↓	Beginning of next paragraph.
PGUP	Top of current screen.
PGDN	Bottom of current screen.
ALT + HOME	Top of current page.
ALT + END	Bottom of current page.
ALT + PGUP	One page up.
ALT + PGDN	One page down.
CTRL + HOME	Beginning of the document.
CTRL + END	End of the document.

Text Selection

MOUSE	KEYBOARD	EXPLANATION
	SHFT + →	One character to the right.
	SHFT + ←	One character to the left.
	CTRL + SHFT + →	To beginning of next word.
	CTRL + SHFT + ←	To beginning of previous word.
	SHFT + END	From insertion point to the end of the line.
	SHFT + HOME	From insertion point to the beginning of the line.
	SHFT + ↑	From insertion point to previous line.
	SHFT + ↓	From insertion point to next line.
	CTRL + SHFT + ↑	From insertion point to beginning of paragraph.
	CTRL + SHFT + ↓	From insertion point to beginning of next paragraph.
Double-click		A word.
Triple-click		A sentence.
Quadruple-click		A paragraph.

Inserting and Deleting

KEYBOARD	EXPLANATION
INS	Toggles between Insert and Typeover modes.
DEL	Erases character at the insertion point, or erases selected text.
BKSP	Erases one character left of the insertion point.
CTRL + BKSP	Erases one word.
CTRL + DEL	Erases from insertion point to the end of the line.

Menus and Commands

The following WordPerfect 6 for Windows commands and keystroke combinations are grouped by menu and listed in the same sequence as they appear on the menu bar in a document window. Commands marked with an asterisk were not discussed in this module.

FILE MENU	MOUSE	KEYBOARD	EXPLANATION
New	🗋	CTRL + N	Creates a new document in a new document window.
Template*		CTRL + T	Creates and opens a pre-designed form for a document.
Open	📂	CTRL + O	Opens an existing file and inserts it into a new document window.
Close		CTRL + F4	Closes the active document window.
Save	💾	CTRL + S	Saves document to disk with current file name.
Save As		F3	Saves document to disk with a different file name.
QuickFinder*			Finds files matching a file name pattern on disk.
Master Document*			Creates links with other documents.
Compare Document*			Shows differences between the current document and a different version of the document.
Document Summary*			Creates descriptive information about a document.
Document Info*			Displays a word count and other information about a document.
Preferences			Changes initial WordPerfect and document settings.
Print	🖨	F5	Prints a document or any portion of a document.
Select Printer			Selects from available printers and changes printer options.
Exit		ALT + F4	Quits WordPerfect.
numbered document names			Opens recently edited documents.

EDIT MENU	MOUSE	KEYBOARD	EXPLANATION
Undo	[icon]	CTRL + Z	Reverses the last change that was made to the document.
Undelete		CTRL + SHFT + Z	Restores the most recent deletions.
Repeat			Sets the number of times to do the next operation.
Cut	[icon]	CTRL + X	Moves selected text to the Clipboard.
Copy	[icon]	CTRL + C	Copies selected text to the Clipboard.
Paste	[icon]	CTRL + V	Inserts Clipboard contents at the insertion point.
Append*			Adds a copy of selected text to the end of the Clipboard.
Select			Selects a sentence, a paragraph, or other block of text.
Paste Special*			Inserts Clipboard contents at the insertion point in the format you choose.
Links*			Creates, views, and cancels links with other documents.
Object*			Opens an embedded or linked object.
Find		F2	Looks for occurrences of a search string in a document.
Replace		CTRL + F2	Looks for and replaces existing text with new text.
Go To		CTRL + G	Moves the insertion point on the page or to a different page.
Convert Case			Changes selected text to uppercase or lowercase.

VIEW MENU	MOUSE	KEYBOARD	EXPLANATION
Draft*		CTRL + F5	Shows text mono-spaced and with no formatting like the screen characteristics in the DOS versions of WordPerfect.
Page		ALT + F5	Shows text with formatting, and with headers and footers.
Two Page			Shows two pages of a document.
Zoom	100% / magnifier icon		Changes the active document window magnification.
Button Bar	button bar icon		Shows or hides the current button bar.
Power Bar			Shows or hides the Power Bar.
Ruler Bar		ALT + SHFT + F3	Shows or hides the Ruler Bar.
Status Bar			Shows or hides the Status Bar.
Hide Bars		ALT + SHFT + F5	Removes or shows all the bars.
Graphics			Shows or hides graphics in a document.
Table Gridlines*			Shows or hides row and column lines in a table.
Hidden Text*			Shows or hides comments and other personal messages in a document.
Show*		CTRL + SHFT + F3	Shows or hides the symbols for space, hard return, tab, and indent in a document.
Reveal Codes		ALT + F3	Shows or hides the embedded codes in the document.

INSERT MENU	MOUSE	KEYBOARD	EXPLANATION
Bullets & Numbers			Places bullet and number characters into a document.
Character		CTRL + W	Chooses and inserts WordPerfect characters into a document.
Abbreviations*			Creates abbreviations of selected text in a document.
Date			Defines and inserts the date into documents.
Other*			Inserts the filename, path, and other information into a document.
Footnote			Creates, edits, and formats footnotes.
Endnote			Creates, edits, formats, and positions endnotes.
Comment*			Creates and modifies comments placed in a document.
Sound*			Creates and edits sound clips placed in a document.
Bookmark*			Marks a location in a document.
Spreadsheet/Database*			Creates links between a document and spreadsheet or database files.
File			Copies a document stored on disk to the active document window.
Object*			Places information created in other Windows applications into a document.
Page Break		CTRL + ENTER	Begins a new page at the insertion point.

LAYOUT MENU	MOUSE	KEYBOARD	EXPLANATION
Font	[FfF] [±A]	F9	Selects the font, appearance, and size of text.
Line			Changes line format.
Paragraph			Changes paragraph format.
Page			Changes page format.
Document*			Changes document format.
Columns	[icon]		Defines, creates, and edits text columns.
Headers/Footers			Creates and edits headers and footers.
Watermark			Places a drawing or clip art image behind the printed text of a document.
Margins		CTRL + F8	Changes left, right, top, and bottom margins.
Justification	[≡L]		Aligns text in a document.
Typesetting*			Adjusts spacing between words and sets other typesetting features.
Envelope			Prints mailing addresses on envelopes.
Labels			Creates and edits mailing lists and other labels.
QuickFormat*			Copies fonts and other text appearance attributes from one area of text to another in a document.
Styles*		ALT + F8	Creates and names a group of text formats to be used in a document.

TOOLS MENU	MOUSE	KEYBOARD	EXPLANATION
Speller	☑	CTRL + F1	Checks for misspelled words, double words, and irregular capitalization.
Thesaurus	⊞	ALT + F1	Displays synonyms and antonyms for a word.
Grammatik*	⊞	ALT + SHFT + F1	Checks text for grammar and style problems.
Language*			Specifies the language of text.
Macro*			Records, edits, and plays macros.
Merge		SHFT + F9	Selects options to create, edit, and perform merges.
Sort*		ALT + F9	Rearranges characters alphabetically or numerically.
Outline*			Creates and edits outlines.
Hypertext*			Turns on Hypertext Feature Bar.
List*			Selects text to be included in a list.
Index*			Selects text to be included in an index.
Cross-Reference*			Selects cross-references in a document.
Table of Contents*			Selects text to be included in the table of contents of a document.
Table of Authorities*			Selects text to be included in a table of authorities of a document.
Generate*		CTRL + F9	Creates and updates the table of contents, cross-references, indexes, table of authorities, lists, and hypertext links in a document.

GRAPHICS MENU	MOUSE	KEYBOARD	EXPLANATION
Figure			Creates and changes a figure box.
Text			Creates and changes a text box.
Equation*			Creates and changes an equation box.
Custom Box*			Creates a custom graphics box.
Edit Box		SHFT + F11	Changes any graphics box.
Draw*			Creates drawings with WP Draw application.
Chart*			Creates charts with WP Draw application.
TextArt*			Creates artwork and special effects with text characters.
Horizontal Line		CTRL + F11	Creates and changes horizontal lines.
Vertical Line		CTRL + SHFT + F11	Creates and changes vertical lines.
Custom Line			Creates a line with selected characteristics.
Edit Line			Changes characteristics of a line.
Graphics Styles*			Creates and names a group of graphics formats to be used in a document.

TABLE MENU	MOUSE	KEYBOARD	EXPLANATION
Create	🔲	F12	Creates a table in a document.
Format		CTRL + F12	Formats cells, rows, and columns in a table.
Number Type		ALT + F12	Formats the numbers in a table.
Lines/Fill		SHFT + F12	Changes the characteristics of lines and cells in a table.
Insert			Places new rows and columns into a table.
Delete			Removes rows, columns, and data from a table.
Join			Combines cells into one cell.
Split			Divides one cell into two or more cells.
Names*			Creates a list of table names.
Calculate			Calculates the value of formulas in a table.
Copy Formula			Replicates a formula in another cell in a table.
Data Fill		CTRL + SHFT + F12	Places data or formulas in cells in a table.
Sum		CTRL + =	Calculates the sum of numbers in a row or column.
Cell Formula Entry			Creates a formula in a cell in a table.
Formula Bar			Turns on Formula Feature Bar.

WINDOW MENU	MOUSE	KEYBOARD	EXPLANATION
Cascade			Arranges document windows so that they overlap with title bars showing.
Tile			Arranges document windows so that each can be seen.
numbered windows			Switches to another document window.

HELP MENU	MOUSE	KEYBOARD	EXPLANATION
Contents			Lists WordPerfect Help topics.
Search For Help On			Shows information on selected topics.
How Do I			Displays information on how to do many procedures.
Macros*			Shows information on using macro commands.
Coach*			Shows step-by-step information on how to do selected procedures.
Tutorial*			Shows short lessons on basic word processing procedures.
About WordPerfect			Shows the product and licence information for WordPerfect installation.

Glossary

absolute tab   A tab setting measured from the left edge of the paper. Text aligned on an absolute tab does not shift if the left margin is changed. *See also* relative tab.

anchor   A graphics box can be anchored or treated as part of a particular character, paragraph, or page.

application Control-menu box   A small rectangular button in the upper left corner of the WordPerfect application window. Clicking will display the Control menu; double-clicking will close the application.

base font   The font that is used to print the characters in a document.

block   A character, word, phrase, sentence, paragraph, or other text selected to be manipulated. A selected block of text is highlighted on the screen. *See also* select.

block operation   Any manipulation of selected text including copying, moving, and deleting text.

boilerplate   Standard passages of text, stored as files, that are repeatedly used in documents. Boilerplate text can be of any length.

button   A graphic representation of a command or an option.

Button Bar   A row of buttons used to quickly access commands that are frequently used.

cell   The intersection of a row and column in a table.

cell address   The column letter and row number of a cell in a table.

character string   Any sequence of characters, including spaces.

check box   Located in dialog boxes and used to toggle an option on or off. If the check box contains an X, the option is turned on.

clip art   Pre-existing artwork or drawings, stored as files on disk, that can be retrieved and inserted into a document.

Clipboard   A temporary storage location used by Windows when copying or moving blocks of text from one location to another.

code   Command inserted into a document to cause the computer to perform a procedure, such as formatting or merging.

column   Text between a left and right margin. *See also* newspaper columns and parallel columns. Also, a group of cells arranged vertically in a table.

command button   Located in dialog boxes and used to continue or cancel a command sequence. It often has a label that describes the action it carries out, such as OK, Cancel, or Help.

context-sensitive Help   Used to display information about whatever feature is currently being used in the document window.

copying text   To duplicate a block of text at another location in the same document or another document.

current document   A document in a document window that will be affected by an operation. Also called the active window.

data file   A document that contains records comprised of fields that represent the variable information that can be merged with a form file to produce a custom document. Also called a list file.

deselect   To clear a selection. *See also* select.

desktop publishing   Word processing features to incorporate text and graphics in a document.

dialog box   A window used to select and implement options, and to display warnings and messages.

document A typed representation of a message, stored on disk as a file.

document Control-menu box Used to exit a document, resize the document window, or switch to another document. Located as a small rectangular button in the upper-left corner of the document window.

document window A window containing a document you create or modify by using WordPerfect for Windows. There can be as many as nine document windows open at any one time. *See also* current document.

dot leaders A series of dots that precede text entered at a tab location.

drop-down list box Located in dialog boxes and used to select from a list of choices that are displayed when the box is chosen.

editing The process of adding, changing, or deleting the contents of a document.

emphasis The aspects of a document's design that attract a reader's attention to particular important ideas in a document.

endnote References, explanations, or comments that are organized and printed at the end of a chapter or document. *See also* footnote.

figure box Used to display a clip art file provided with WordPerfect 6 for Windows or graphic images created in other applications. *See also* graphics box.

file A document that has been given a name and stored on disk.

file operation Any manipulation of a file as a whole, including saving to and retrieving from disk.

fixed information Text that is intended to be the same for all the recipients of a document. *See also* variable information.

font The particular typeface, style, and size attributes of printed characters.

footer A block of text printed at the bottom of each page in a document. *See also* header.

footnote A reference, explanation, or comment printed at the end of a page in a document. *See also* endnote.

form file A document file containing fixed information and merge codes that control how text from a data file, boilerplate files, and the keyboard are combined to produce a custom document.

format To arrange the text of a document for the printed page. Some formatting techniques include setting margins, tabs, line spacing, page breaks, and centering and indenting text.

formatting Arranging the text for the printed page to attract the reader's attention to important ideas in the document and to improve the readability of the document.

formatting code A code used to control how text appears on the printed page. *See also* code.

formula A mathematical expression entered in a cell of a table.

global search and replace To scan an entire document, replacing every occurrence of a character string with a new character string. *See also* search. *See also* search and replace.

graphics box A rectangular area you can define in a document to display text, clip art, tables, equations, or other graphics. *See also* text box, figure box.

Graphics Box Feature Bar A horizontal bar containing buttons to select options that are frequently used to create and edit graphic boxes in a document.

hard page break A code placed in a document to cause text to continue to the next page prior to the normal end of a page. *See also* soft page break.

header A block of text printed at the top of each page in a document. *See also* footer.

header record The first record in a data file that lists the names of the fields in the order in which they appear in each record.

headword A word in the Thesaurus that has additional synonyms and antonyms.

I-beam pointer The shape of the pointer when it is positioned in the work area of a document window.

Image Tools palette A group of fourteen buttons for editing images in a graphics box.

indenting   Using a tab location as the left margin for a block of text until [ENTER] is pressed.

Insert mode   Characters entered into a document at the insertion point shift existing text to the right. *See also* typeover mode.

insertion point   The place where text will be inserted when you type. The insertion point usually appears as a flashing vertical bar. The text you type appears to the left of the insertion point, which is pushed to the right as you type.

jump term   Words and phrases in Help windows that display information on related topics. Jump terms are highlighted and underlined.

justification   The alignment of text within the left and/or right margins.

line spacing   The white space between lines of text.

list box   Located in dialog boxes and used to list available choices.

margin   The space between the text area of a document and the top, bottom, and side edges of the paper.

margin markers   The top row of the Ruler Bar indicating the left and right margin settings.

Maximize button   Used to enlarge a window to its maximum size. Located at the right end of the title bar and displayed as a single up arrow. *See also* restore button.

menu bar   A horizontal bar across the top part of a document window containing the ten main headings for the WordPerfect for Windows menus.

merge code   Used to control how information is retrieved from a data file, boilerplate file, or the keyboard and inserted into a form file. Merge codes are inserted in form and data files.

merging   To combine information from two or more source documents into one target document.

Minimize button   Used to shrink a window to an icon. Located at the right end of the title bar and displayed as a single down arrow. *See also* Restore button.

moving text   To relocate a block of text from one position in a document to another position in the same document or to another document.

newspaper columns   Vertical columns of text on the page in which text runs from top to bottom in the leftmost column and then wraps to the top of the next column to the right. *See also* column.

paragraph   Any size block of text that is ended by pressing [ENTER].

parallel columns   Vertical columns of text on the page in which text entered in one column is kept aligned with text in other columns. *See also* column.

pop-up terms   Words and phrases in Help windows that display their definition when selected. Pop-up terms are highlighted with a dotted underline.

Power Bar   A row of buttons to select the most frequently used text editing and text layout commands. The Power Bar can be customized to include buttons to select other word processing commands. When the Power Bar is toggled on, it is located across the upper part of a document window.

preview window   Located in dialog boxes to show how editing changes will look in the document.

pull-down menu   The menu associated with each of the ten main headings on the menu bar.

radio button   Located in dialog boxes and used to select one item in a group of mutually exclusive items.

readability   The aspects of a document's design that relate to how well a reader understands the meaning of the author's message.

relative tab   A tab setting measured from the left margin. Text aligned on a relative tab shifts if the left margin is changed. *See also* absolute tab.

Restore button   Used to return a document window that has been maximized to a smaller size; located at the right end of the menu bar and displayed as a small box with a up/down arrow. Also used to return an application window to a smaller size; located at the right end of the title bar and displayed as a small box with an up/down arrow. *See also* Maximize button.

Reveal Codes bar   A horizontal double line dividing the document window into two areas. The text of the current document is displayed in both areas, with any formatting codes also displayed in the lower area.

row   A group of cells arranged horizontally across a table.

Ruler Bar   A horizontal bar that displays the settings for the left and right margins and tabs. When the Ruler Bar is toggled on, it is located across the upper part of a document window.

sans serif typeface   A set of characters that do not have small cross lines, or serifs, at the bottom end strokes of each letter. *See also* serif typeface.

scale   The horizontal and vertical dimensions of a graphics image.

scroll bar   Used to move a document up and down, or left and right, to view text that does not fit on the screen. Located at the right and/or bottom edge of some document windows.

scrolling   To move a document up and down, or left and right, to view text that cannot fit on the screen.

search and replace   To scan a document for a character, word, phrase, or code, and replace it with another character, word, phrase, or code.

select   To identify a file, block of text, graphics box, or other item that will be affected by subsequent actions. Also, to identify a dialog box option to be applied to a file, block of text, graphics box, or other item. *See also* deselect.

serif typeface   A set of characters that have small cross lines, or serifs, at the bottom end strokes of each letter. *See also* sans serif typeface.

sizing handles   The small solid squares that appear on the borders of a graphics box that has been selected. You can drag these handles to change the size of the box.

soft page break   A [SPg] code indicating that text automatically continues on the next page. *See also* hard page break.

source document   A document containing text to be copied or moved to another document. *See also* target document.

spell checking   To verify the spelling of a word, block of text, or an entire document.

Speller   The spell-checking feature in WordPerfect 6 for Windows.

status bar   Displays the position of the insertion point in the document and other information and messages when WordPerfect is performing certain functions. Located at the bottom edge of a document window.

subheading   Text used as a title for a specific portion of a document to divide the document into visual units to improve the document's readability.

superscript   A character positioned slightly above other characters on the same line.

tab marker   The location of a particular tab setting on the ruler.

tab setting   Control the position of text from the left margin when TAB is pressed or the text is indented.

table   Information displayed in a row-and-column format. *See also* row, column.

target document   A document into which text is inserted from another document. *See also* source document.

text box   1. Located in dialog boxes and used to type information needed to carry out a command. 2. A graphics box used to display text. *See also* graphics box.

Thesaurus   A WordPerfect feature to replace a word in your document with another word from a list of synonyms and antonyms.

title bar   A horizontal bar across the top of a window indicating the name of the application and/or document in which you are working.

toggle   A word processing feature that turns on and off with the same command.

type size   The vertical measurement of characters measured in points, where one point is 1/72 of an inch. *See also* font.

type style   The special characteristics of a typeface including boldface, italics, underlining, and superscripting and subscripting. *See also* font.

typeface   The design and shape of a set of characters. *See also* font.

Typeover mode   Characters that are entered into a document replace existing characters at the insertion point. *See also* Insert mode.

variable information   Text that changes from one document to another, depending on the recipient of the document. *See also* fixed information.

white space   Blank areas around text to provide a visual contrast so the document does not look crowded.

window   A rectangular area on the screen in which you view an application or document. *See also* document window.

word processing   Using a computer to create, edit, store, retrieve, and print documents.

word wrap   A word processing feature that automatically moves text from the end of a line to the beginning of a new line as you type.

work area   The portion of the document window where a document is displayed as you type and edit.

Index

Absolute tabs, 80. *See also* Tabs
Aligning text, 71-75
`ALT`, 11
Antonyms, 50-52
Arrow keys, 11, 26-27

Base font, 96
`BKSP`, 28-29
Blocks, text, 54. *See also* Text
Boldface text, 97, 98
Button Bar, 9, 12, 14. *See also specific function*

Cancelling commands, 11
Centering text, 73, 74-75
Characters, WordPerfect, 98-100
Character strings, 47
Check boxes, 13
Clipboard, 57
Close command, 19, 35
Codes
 formatting, 66-68
Command buttons (in dialog boxes), 12, 13
Commands. *See also specific command or function*
 Button Bar, 9, 12, 14
 cancelling and undoing, 11
 choosing from keyboard, 11
 choosing with mouse, 10-11
 dialog boxes in, 12-15
 Feature bars. *See* Feature bars
 list of, 118-126
 Power Bar, 8, 9, 12
Context-sensitive Help, 15, 17
Control-menu box, 8, 9, 19
Copying text, 57-58, 115
`CTRL`, 11
Cut command, 56-57

Decimal alignment, 75, 76
Definitions, pop-up, 15, 16, 18
Deleting
 formatting codes, 67
 tabs, 77-78
 text, 28-29, 55-56

Deselecting text, 55
Desktop publishing, 6
Dialog boxes, 10, 12-15. *See also specific function*
Directories, in document opening, 44
Documents. *See also specific component*
 copying text between, 115
 exiting, 35
 inserting one in another, 115
 maximum open simultaneously, 115
 navigating within, 26-28
 opening, 43-45
 page breaks in, 84-86
 saving. *See* Saving documents
 sizing, 32-33
 spell checking, 50-52
 switching between, 115
 text in. *See* Text
 viewing before opening, 45
 white space in, 64
Document window, 6, 7-9
Dot leaders, 75, 78-79
Drop-down list boxes, 12

Edit menu, 9, 119. *See also specific command or function*
`END`, 27
Endnotes, 95, 104-106
`ENTER`
 in choosing commands, 11
 in separating paragraphs, 25-26
`ESC`, 11
Exiting
 documents, 35
 WordPerfect, 19

`F1`, 17
Feature bars
 footnote/endnote, 104-106
 header/footer, 102-103
Figure boxes, 114

File menu, 9, 116-117. *See also specific command or function*
Files. *See* Documents
Finding and replacing text, 47-49
Fonts
 base, 96
 changing, 96-97, 103, 106
 overview and components, 93-94
Footers, 95, 102-103
Footnotes, 95, 104-106
Foreign language characters, 98-100
Formatting
 codes, 66-68
 indents, 81-83
 justification, 71-75
 line spacing, 83-84
 margins, 69-71
 overview, 64
 page breaks, 84-86
 Ruler Bar, 9, 10-11, 68-69
 tabs. *See* Tabs
Full justification, 71-72

Global search and replace, 49
Glossary buttons, 17, 18
Graphical user interface, 6
Graphics, 114
Graphics menu, 124
GUI, 6

Hanging indents, 81, 82-83
Hard page breaks, 84-86
Headers, 95, 102-103
Headwords, 52
Help
 context-sensitive, 17
 displaying general information about, 15-16
 keystroke combinations for, 116
 menu for, 9, 126
 overview, 15
 searching, 18-19
History button, 17
`HOME`, 27

I-beam pointer, 8
Iconic symbols, 98-100

Indenting text, 81-83. *See also* Ruler Bar; Tabs
Insertion point
 described, 5, 8
 moving in documents, 26-28
Insert menu, 9, 121. *See also specific command or function*
Insert mode, 28
`INS`, 28
Italics, 97, 98

Jump terms, 15-17
Justifying text, 71-75

Keystroke combinations, 11, 116-117. *See also specific function*

Layout menu, 9, 122. *See also specific function*
Leaders, 75, 78-79
Left justification, 71-75
Line command, 74
Line spacing, 83-84. *See also* Ruler Bar
List boxes, 12, 13-15

Margins, 69-71. *See also* Indenting text; Ruler Bar
Mathematics, symbols, 98-100
Maximize button, 8
Menus
 items in. *See* Commands
 menu bar, 8, 9
 overview, 8-11
Minimize button, 8
Mouse pointer, 8. *See also* Insertion point
Moving text, 56-58, 115

Numbering pages, 100-101

Open command, 43-45

Pages
 breaks in, 84-86
 footnotes and endnotes, 95, 104-106
 headers and footers, 95, 102-103
 numbering, 100-101

Paragraphs. *See* Text
Paste command, 56-57
`PGUP` and `PGDN`, 27
Pop-up terms, 15, 16, 18
Power Bar, 8, 9, 12. *See also* specific function
Previewing documents, 32-33
Preview windows, 13
Printing
  basic procedure, 34
  preview, 32-33
Pull-down menus, 10

Quadruple-clicking, 55
Quitting WordPerfect for Windows, 19

Radio buttons, 13
Relative tabs, 80
Replacing text
  finding and, 47-49
  with Speller, 50-51
Restore button, 8
Reveal Codes feature, 66-68
Right justification, 72
Rows. *See* Tables
Ruler Bar, 9, 10-11, 68-69. *See also* Line spacing; Margins; Tabs

Sans serif, vs. serif, 93-94
Save As command, 45-46
Saving documents
  after first time, 32
  first time, 30-31
  to new document, 115
  recommended frequency of, 32
  under another name, 45-46
  upon exiting, 35
Scientific symbols, 98-100
Scrolling, 5, 8, 9
Searching
  for Help topics, 18-19
  for text, and replacing, 47-49
Selecting
  text, 54-55
Serif, vs. sans serif, 93-94
Sizing
  documents, 32-33
  text, 96-97
  windows, 8
Soft page breaks, 85
Special characters, 98-100
Spell checking, 6, 50-52

Starting WordPerfect for Windows, 7-8
Status bar, 8, 9
Subheadings, 64
Superscripts, 94
Symbols, 98-100
Synonyms, 50-52

`TAB`
  in advancing to tabs. *See* Tabs
  in choosing commands, 14-15
  in using Help, 16, 18
Tables
  lines in, 115
  menu for, 9, 125
  overview, 114, 115
Tabs. *See also* Indenting text; Ruler Bar
  absolute vs. relative, 80
  clearing, 77-78
  inserting, 77
  overview and types, 69, 75-77
  setting, 78-81
Text. *See also* Documents; Footers; Headers
  boldface, 97, 98
  copying, 57-58, 115
  deleting, 28-29, 55-56
  entering, 25-26, 28
  finding and replacing, 47-49
  fonts. *See* Fonts
  formatting. *See* Formatting
  as graphic element. *See* Text boxes
  indenting, 81-83. *See also* Ruler Bar; Tabs
  italics, 97, 98
  moving, 56-58, 115
  in page numbers, 100-101
  readability and emphasis, 42
  selecting and deselecting, 54-55, 117
  serif, vs. sans serif, 93-94
  special characters, 98-100
  in tables. *See* Tables
  wrapping, 5
Text box (in dialog boxes), 12-13
Thesaurus, 6, 52-54
Title bar, 8
Tools menu, 9, 123. *See also* specific command or function

Triple-clicking, 55
Typeface and type size. *See* Fonts
Typeover mode, 28

Undeleting text, 56
Underlining text, 98
Undoing commands, 11

Viewer window, 45
View menu, 9, 120. *See also* specific command or function

White space, 64
Window menu, 9, 126
Windows. *See also* Documents
  arranging multiple, 115
  definition, 18
  document, 6, 7-9
  preview, 13
  sizing, 8
  switching between, 8, 9, 115
WordPerfect for Windows. *See also* Word processors
  exiting, 19
  overview, 6
  starting, 7-8
WordPerfect Characters, 98-100
Word processors, 1, 5-6. *See also* WordPerfect for Windows
Word wrap, 5
Work area, 8

Zoom feature, 32-33